African American Christian Worship

Melva Wilson Costen

Abingdon Press
Nashville

AFRICAN AMERICAN CHRISTIAN WORSHIP

Library of Congress Cataloging-in-Publication Data

Costen, Melva Wilson, 1933-
    African American Christian worship / Melva Wilson Costen.—Rev. ed.
        p. cm.
    Includes bibliographical references and index.
    ISBN 978-0-687-64622-7 (pbk. : alk. paper)
    1. African American public worship. I Title.

    BR563.N4C68 2007
    264.0089'96073—dc22

                                                                2007013641

07 08 09 10 11 12 13 14 15 16—10 9 8 7 6 5 4 3 2 1
MANUFACTURED IN THE UNITED STATES OF AMERICA

AFRICAN AMERICAN CHRISTIAN WORSHIP

In memory of my parents, John Theodore Wilson and Azzie Lee Ellis Wilson, who taught me what it means to live a liturgical life

In memory of my husband, James Hutten Costen Sr.

For our children:
James Hutten Jr., Craig Lamont, and Cheryl Leatrice

Our grandchildren:
Josef Costen, Erica Costen, Jordan Costen, Maranda Costen, Zettler Clay IV, and Takara Clay

Our great-grandchildren:
JaMeah Costen, Jaedon Costen, and JaKira Costen

CONTENTS

ACKNOWLEDGMENTS

This book emerged over a period of years out of a need for historical resources that trace the merger and planting of African religious ancestry and Christian faith traditions on North American soil. The harsh slave soil was transformed by the Almighty into fertile landscapes, enabling and nurturing a diversity of forms and styles of worship, uniquely *African American*. I am grateful for the support of my liturgical colleagues in theological seminaries, universities, and colleges who encouraged this publication and were first to add it to their class syllabi. From the walls of the academy, *African American Christian Worship* has become a major resource at national worship and music conferences, in local congregations, and in educational institutions in African countries where English is read and spoken. For this I am grateful, especially to former students and recent graduates of the Interdenominational Theological Center.

I am deeply indebted to my parents, who brought me to the baptismal font, and to the community of faith from a diversity of African American denominational traditions, who stood with us at the font in Due West, South Carolina, and participated in the early nurturing process. I also owe a debt of gratitude to my stepmother, Nelsie T. Johnson, who entered my life during the crucial adolescent years and continues her parental nurturing as she moves into her ninety-fifth year as a worship leader and church musician.

I am grateful for the love and support of my late husband, James H. Costen Sr., whose companionship facilitated the African data-gathering and writing processes; my children, who continually experience the African connections; my siblings, who encouraged me to record the worship legacy that shaped us; and my six grandchildren and three great-grandchildren, who are God's gracious gifts and constant reminders that the legacy of love and faith continues.

Special thanks to Abingdon Press for the opportunity to revise and enlarge the contents of this book where needed, and especially for the support of Kathy Armistead and Susan Cornell for editorial assistance.

A CALL TO WORSHIP

The sound of "talking drums" permeated the halls and campus of the Interdenominational Theological Center. It was 10:40 AM, twenty minutes before the regularly scheduled chapel hour, and the entire community was called to worship in a language that was especially familiar to the large African seminary constituency. Students in the worship class automatically followed the lead of African students as they assumed an attitude of prayer. After a moment of silence, the assignment for the next session was given and the class was dismissed.

When the community gathered for worship, the nonverbal call to praise was alternated with verbal phrases in an antiphonal reminder of the freedom of Almighty God to speak in tongues of humans and all of creation! Without any explanation, the community experienced reminders of the power and greatness of God, who is to be praised with loud clashing cymbals (and drums). With skillful artistry, the drummers echoed words of the psalmist in gradually diminishing tones: "Worship the Lord in holy array; tremble before God, all the earth!" In songs, words, and prayers from a variety of races and cultures, the diverse community was unified in the worship of God in Jesus Christ. By God's initiative, people from a variety of places on the earth had accepted the invitation to enter into God's story where they were, had claimed the biblical heritage, and were able to hear one another as they worshiped in "holy array"!

CHAPTER 1

A THEOLOGY OF AFRICAN AMERICAN WORSHIP

African American Christians gathered and engaged in worship, regardless of denomination, share many things in common. First and foremost, they gather to offer thanks and praise to God in and through Jesus the Christ, and to be spiritually fed by the Word of God! In response to God's call and by God's grace, communities of faith gather to affirm God's providence and power. Under the power of the Holy Spirit, African Americans express their corporate and personal belief that God in Jesus Christ continues to work for good in every aspect of their lives. There is an ethos of beloved community as the "extended family" recalls and celebrates freedom in Christ. Aware of the mysterious presence of the living Christ, the community is empowered to live the good news in the world.

Second, they share the reality of a common historical taproot, which extends deep into the nurturing center of the African soil. The community of faith can attest to the strength and sturdiness of this root by the nurturing it continues to provide Africans in diaspora. Although the African heritage is not a monolithic entity, there are shared African primal world views that provide fundamental ways of knowing and experiencing God. For most African societies, humans live in a religious universe, so that natural phenomena, objects, and all of life are associated with acts of God.[1] Life is thus viewed holistically rather than in separate compartments as created by a secular-sacred dichotomy. These world views and other aspects of African cultures continued to exist as new world views and cultures were developing. Although languages, religions, customs, and institutions were diverse, many African societies shared certain virtues, ideals, cultural expressions, and outlooks on past, present, and future, which provided spiritual armor capable of surviving the impact of slavery.

1

Some branches of the African heritage include direct involvement in the shaping of Judeo-Christian worship traditions. From the time Abraham came out of Ur and settled in Egypt, through the time when the church wrestled with the formulation of theological statements and the shaping of significant creeds, Africa has played a critical role. Nine Africans were among the prominent leaders in this struggle: Clement, Origen, Tertullian, Cyprian, Dionysius, Athanasius, Didymus, Augustine, and Cyril.

A third common particularity of African Americans gathered for worship is their history of struggle for survival as African people in America. In a strange and alien land, they were enslaved, marginalized, denied respect, and oppressed by the very people who introduced them to Christianity! This unique history allows the gathered Christian community to freely call itself by whatever name it chooses. African American, Black, and Afro-American have replaced the names spuriously given by Euro-American evangelizers. This history also served to deepen the need for communities of refuge, which happen naturally when people gather around a common cause. The gathered community, first in secrecy as "invisible communities of faith," found that the separate environments were conducive to authentic communication with God and with one another.

There was little if any concern during this early period for adherence to denominational polity, recitation of creeds, or "acceptable" employment of superimposed, predetermined liturgical actions. There was concern for the exposition and hearing of biblical truths that had meaning for an enslaved people. Since the Word of God was heard in their particular contexts, responses were very often spontaneous reflections of the primal world views still very much alive. Symbols and ritual actions were gradually shaped around socially shared patterns, customs, and forms, with an apparent awareness of the human need to respond with one's whole being!

The "invisible" environment allowed free space, God's space, where enslaved worshipers could hear an anticipated message of hope in God's word. The personhood of each worshiper could be affirmed. The community could experience freedom—divine freedom—in Christ. Each time a member of the community of faith experienced freedom from bondage or a physical healing moment, the total community would vicariously experience a newfound freedom. Conversion experiences and baptisms were important times for the communal sharing of faith. The spiritual gifts and artistic talents of individuals that edified the community were acknowledged and encouraged in worship. In separate, sacred spaces, gifts and talents were not subjected to evaluation and scrutiny by Europeans and Americans. Worship gatherings, especially where elements of the oral tradition are at work, are opportunities for the community of faith to continually reconstitute and reinforce the spiritual bond within and between congregations.

Under the power of the Holy Spirit, a new theology was forged and flamed while the church worshiped. The methodology used was honed from "folk methods" common to Africans and transported wherever Africans are in diaspora. Music, song, and storytelling by the *griot* (a West African term for "one who is gifted in the art of communicating wisdom, ideas, historical events, morals, etc.") became the major means of shaping, documenting, and distributing folk theology. This common heritage continues to be a channel through which the Spirit of God edifies and empowers the body of Christ. Gathered and scattered as African American Christians in the present age, believers are provided sustenance by this rich heritage that propels believers, with hope, into the future.

From the African taproot, the early shapers of Black folk religion forged a Christian world view, or "sacred cosmos," that permeates all of life.[2] Everyday living is not separate from worship. The reality of human corruption, oppression, and inequality anywhere in the world provides a hermeneutical principle, a lens through which the Word of God is seen, heard, understood, felt, and interpreted in worship.

Although African Americans share many common worship practices, one should not assume that *all* African American congregations will or should exhibit homogeneous styles of worship. Different situations and circumstances under which exposure to Christianity took place for each congregation, denomination (history and theological orientation), geography, and social lifestyles are significant determinants of worship.

The traditional manner of "labeling" denominational differences among African American worshipers has not always been accurate, nor has it been helpful. The stereotyping of ritual action has not always taken into consideration the sociological factors of cross-ritual assimilation between denominations, especially in small communities in the South. There are also differences in ritual action *within* denominations. To assume, for instance, that all African American Presbyterians should be numbered among the "frozen-chosen" is to ignore the dynamics of

"Spirit-filled" churches such as those in rural sections of North and South Carolina and Georgia. To claim that *all* African American Baptist worship services are highly emotional is to negate the "modulated" liturgical experiences and expressions of *some* African American Baptists in both urban and rural settings. The trend from the late 1960s forward among some African American congregations traditionally labeled "frozen," "staid," or "unemotional" has been toward a more expressive worship.[3] Some African American Catholic, Episcopalian, United Methodist, Disciples of Christ, United Church of Christ, Lutheran, and Presbyterian worshipers are rediscovering and reclaiming their common Afrocentric theological roots. More will be said about this in a later chapter.

Core Beliefs

The common elements of history and traditions provide a starting point for a discourse on African American liturgical theology. Whereas different denominational polities may indeed affect the ordering of worship elements, many liturgical practices originated from basic beliefs of African peoples. Some of the ritual action that may appear to be an adherence to the institutional practices of Western-oriented theologies may, in fact, be based on certain African practices that have been transmitted through the oral tradition. This is one indication that many core beliefs remain operative across denominational lines.

We are indebted to the oral and written records of African Americans who attempted to interpret the meaning of the Christian faith amid the struggles for liberation in America. The faith stories of individuals and communities are the major sources of African American theology. We are equally indebted to the rigorous efforts of African American scholars who continue to research and publish significant data needed to theologize from *within* the African American experience.

The concept of "Black Theology," which emerged during the second half of the 1960s, stimulated sufficient African/African American ecumenical dialogue to affirm common threads of history and theology.[4] Since the 1960s, African American scholars in a variety of academic disciplines have continued to contribute to the discussion evolving from the question, What does it mean to be African American and Christian? Documentation gathered from personal trips to Africa and from African scholars supports the thesis that the African taproot is not only deep but is also very much alive and being nurtured by African Americans in worship and life. Theological reflections and publications in a variety of academic disciplines in African American seminaries provide opportunities for reflection-praxis continuity between lived realities and "the academy."[5]

A holistic approach is required for examining worship from within the African American experience. African peoples perceive reality as one related whole rather than as separate compartments. There is no separation of secular and sacred. The "rhythm of life" is bound up in the cosmos—a harmonious world, created and ordered by Almighty God. People of African descent were thinking holistically long before Teilhard de Chardin constructed a Christian cosmogony as a synthesis of love for God bound to love for the world.[6] While postmodernist schools of thought are now returning to the interrelatedness of disciplines in theologizing, folk beliefs that issue from the "soul of Black folks" have continuously reflected this method of theologizing.[7]

African "primordial," or primal, world views that shaped foundational belief systems also undergird African American theologies of worship. World views determine and affect cultural symbols and symbolisms through which beliefs are expressed and transmitted. Prevailing African cosmological views can be summarized as follows:

—God created an orderly world and remains present and is dynamically involved in ongoing creation throughout the inhabited world.

—Human beings are part of God's creation and are, therefore, divinely linked, related to, and involved with all of creation. This cosmological perspective allows an understanding of being (ontology) that is relational and communal.

—An understanding of the "sacred cosmos" that is relevant for the individual must be internalized if one is to find meaning and purpose in life.

—Communal solidarity is expressed in terms of kinship and extended family, both vertically and horizontally.

—Bound by an understanding of the sacredness of God's creation, humans relate holistically to God, to one another, to the cosmos, and to plant and animal life.

—Cosmic rhythm is the embodiment of divine order, harmony, and permanence; cosmic rhythm is the foundation for the "rhythm of life."

Although there are some differences in understandings of the presence and activity of God, creation is undoubtedly the work of God.[8] The cosmos, God's divine creation, is understood as a whole unit or body that is alive, sacred, and the foundation of religious values. Modalities of the sacred and of being are revealed through the natural world and cosmic rhythms. The harmonious structure of the cosmos is a means by which God's transcendence is remembered. "Divine connectedness" is activated through symbols and symbolism. Water, for instance, symbolizes the origin and sustenance of life as well as death and rebirth. Contact with water signifies a return or reincorporation into creation or precreation.[9]

African peoples respond to God's presence in a variety of ways. Responses may be formal or informal, spontaneous or regularized, personal or communal. Worship is generally expressed vocally and physically rather than meditationally.[10] Beliefs as well as ritual actions are related to the lived experiences of the community. Worship is more experiential than rationalistic. Its focus is on the communal sharing of reality rather than simply the transmission of information. Since the focus is primarily experiential, common symbols, shaped by the community, are the major means of communication. Through symbols the community expresses what might be difficult to verbalize. Symbols help "free" the mind of clutter so that clarity can be given to phenomena that might otherwise be incomprehensible. Music, movement, physical gestures, colors, shapes, and the gifts of nature common to the community are very important symbols.

A composite of basic beliefs based on primordial, or "primal," world views has emerged as African Americans make deliberate efforts to theologize from within the African American experience. "Primal" is understood as fundamental or "a priori" rather than the usual concept of "primitive" or undeveloped. Primal beliefs refer to those forms of comprehensive reference-systems that are observable among a variety of religions, and may have been basic to the overall religious history of humankind. All cultures have convictions of reality that are based on traditional ways that the particular world is viewed in the light of circumstances. Thus it is the contention of African American liturgical theology that African primal world views, which lie buried within persons and communities of faith, coexist with and remain operable in Christian theology. In fact, for the African American, the adapting of Christian beliefs necessitated a recasting of concepts taught to an enslaved people, in understandable, functional terms.

Nicholas C. Cooper-Lewter and Henry H. Mitchell are helpful in their exploration of the African American belief systems through case studies of "core beliefs" in action. They contend:

> Core beliefs are much more than easily mouthed shibboleths or conformist creeds. They are bedrock attitudes that govern all deliberate behavior and relationships and also spontaneous responses to crises . . . if indeed . . . expressed at all, core beliefs are our working out opinions about whether God can be trusted. . . . The issue is not the correctness of formulation but the adequacy of trust of the Creator.[11]

A persistent negative attitude toward African primal religions has made it difficult to acknowledge the inheritance of primal world views and core beliefs. Nevertheless, there are sufficient data to substantiate the "primal" acceptance of the unity and wholeness of life, which is evident in African American communal life, religion and worship, music, art, politics, and culture. The outward expressions of feelings and emotions, the tendency to "move with the beat," the similarity of music for worship and music for entertainment all speak to the functioning of an underlying belief system. A system of beliefs imposed by the dominant culture could not and cannot be a viable belief system for a marginalized people. A belief system, already well established in African traditions, continues to help an oppressed community find meaning and make sense of life, maintain community identity and continuity, find direction, and provide healing and empowerment.[12]

Unlike the Western-oriented Christian, whose theology is rooted in Greco-Roman concepts and culture, African peoples tend to seek to *know* God personally rather than to *know about* God from doctrines and creeds. Traditional Africans, whose entire existence is a religious phenomenon, would become immersed early in the idea that God "is," not because they had been told about God's existence, but because God can be experienced in all of creation. This is summarized in the Ashanti proverb: "No one shows a child the Supreme Being," which means in essence that everybody, including children, knows God almost as if by instinct.[13] Christian faith, for traditional Africans, does not mean that one has to assent to or recite certain written doctrines or creeds to prove that one knows about God. What matters is that one seeks to know God through God's revelational activity in one's own life and in the life of the community.

African peoples in America expressed in a number of ways the importance of experiencing and knowing God in Jesus Christ. Personal revelations were so important for some slaves that the reading of the Bible was often deferred until after their conversions. The language of some of the slave songs reveals the biblical message taught in relation to their own experiences. "I heard from heaven today"; "Jesus goin' make up my dying bed"; and "God don't never change" are a few of the many examples. Worship and praise services were especially important to the slaves, for it was here that the encounter between God and humans became real for them. In gospel songs, African Americans continue to document the importance of knowing God. The language of these songs reflects a reaching out through space and time as singers identify with the lived experiences of others, so that the characters, scenes, and events of the Bible become present and provide evidence of hope.

The story is told of a slave who was unable to read and, therefore, relied on others to share the biblical stories. When approached about the depth of her understanding of the gospel message, she replied: "I can't read a word. But I read Jesus in my heart. . . . I knows he's there 'cause I read him in my heart, just like you know about him from reading the book!"

Knowing happens deep within the "soul-roots" of perception as a result of experience. Knowing provides clarity and certainty, which may not lend itself to systematic discourse or to the formulation of hammered-out creeds that might be challenged by Western theology. African American preachers express what the Word of God calls them *to know*, and further authenticate this by recalling the exact experience of the "knowing moment." Hearers participate in and claim the reality of another's "experienced knowledge" as they seek to know for themselves.

Kinship

One of the strongest forces in traditional African life that continues among African Americans is a deep sense of kinship or relatedness. From the perspective of primal world views, God is the continuing source and sustenance of all that is good. Since God called forth the cosmos as an orderly, complete, and perfect entity, all creation and the inhabited universe are sacred to God. Humanity is part of the created order, thus human beings are to exist in unity with one another and with all of creation. To be human means that one belongs to a family or community. The Akan in West Africa express this idea in this manner: Onipe fi soro besi a, obesi nnipa krom, which is freely translated "When a person descends from heaven, he or she enters a town inhabited by human beings." The implication is that society is the context of human existence. One's humanity is defined by a sense of belonging, for it is not enough to be a human being unless one participates in and demonstrates a sense of community. Religion, understood as one with life, is not an isolated part of the community's life, but permeates every facet of the community's existence.

Nearly all concepts connected with the interrelatedness of God's total creation can be understood and interpreted through a hermeneutic of "the kinship system." The sense of kinship is not limited to human relations. It involves all that binds humans to one another and extends to include all of nature—both animal and plant life. Kinship is the basis for an understanding of the community as both the living, the "living-dead" (the deceased who are alive in the memories of the surviving family), and those yet unborn "who are still in the loins of the living."[14] The anticipated arrival of future generations yet unborn provides hope in the continuation of God's ongoing family. A visible symbol of unity, of extended family, of belongingness, togetherness, and common affinity is made possible, according to John S. Mbiti, through the kinship system.

> The kinship system is like a vast network stretching laterally (horizontally) in every direction, to embrace everybody in any given local group. This means that each individual is a brother or sister, father or mother, grandmother or grandfather . . . to everybody else. That means that everybody is related to everybody else . . . it also extends vertically to include the departed . . . and those yet to be born.[15]

This understanding of community created by the kinship system is a reminder that individuals exist as a part of the corporate whole. One becomes aware of self, duties, privileges, and responsibilities in terms of others. A cardinal point in the understanding of this African view of community is the adage: "I am, because we are; and since we are, therefore I am."[16]

It is conceivable that the African concept of kinship provides a foundation for relatedness in the household or family of God in Jesus Christ.

In spite of separation and transition through slavery, this concept continued. New relationships were developed where two or three were gathered in worship or at work. The African community-kinship emerged wherever relationships, based on mutual interdependence, trust, and suffering, took place. African American worship continues as an arena where a people, already related by the Providence of God, can hear the healing Word of God and respond. The unique forms of liturgy in African American worship are the results of what Victor Turner refers to as "anti-structures."[17] Turner contends that anti-structure, as generated through the ritual process, is marginal, but part of the "serious life." Worship as ritual provides an opportunity to create new symbols, which produce structures and anti-structures. Turner argues that

> marginality, and structural inferiority are conditions in which are frequently generated myths, symbols, rituals, philosophical systems, and works of art. These cultural forms provide [us] with a set of . . . models which are, at one level, periodical reclassifications of reality and [our] relationship to society, nature and culture, but they are more than classifications, since they incite [us] to action as well as thought.[18]

In the context of a loving community, the ritual action of worship allows the worshiper to transcend social structures imposed by the dominant culture, thus generating anti-structures. Under the empowerment of the Holy Spirit, freedom is granted and new meaning is given to life. One's dignity and worth are affirmed, a positive self-image can be developed and maintained, and healing can take place. Worshipers hear the Word of God in Jesus Christ as it speaks directly to the realities of their lives and empowers them to live as whole persons in the world.

The worship of African American Christians is informed by at least four streams of tradition: traditional African primal world views; Judeo-Christian religion; African American folk religion, which emanated from world views shaped in the American context in a crisis of slavery and oppression; and Western/Euro-American Christianity. African American *leitourgia* (liturgy)—the work of the people as ritual action, ministry, and service—is reflective of the experiences of a particular people deeply aware of the power and the promise of God.

In accordance with the basic theological foundation upon which worship in the African American community is built, diversity in worship practices can be expected. One must keep in mind that individual African American worshiping communities did not develop overnight.

They evolved over a period of time, with initial beginnings, perhaps, as secret worshipers continuing their African traditions, gradually adding concepts of the Christian faith as described in chapter 3. Once established, the extent to which a congregation reflected all four "streams of traditions" cited above depended upon the location of the congregation (north or south), the composition of the gathered community (slave or free), and the style of the worship leaders. Beyond the period of slavery, the streams of traditions took on new life according to the closeness to or distance removed from the marginal slave environment through which the congregation emerged. More specifically, each congregation established and altered its own worship style, with pastoral leadership but largely controlled by the community. It would be unfair and inaccurate to assume that all Black worship began as duplicate copies of one another. The extent to which communal kinship and cohesiveness are evident would be one of the best measures of the presence of the African world view.

One should also keep in mind that life takes on new meaning in the context of worship in a particular place and at a particular time as divinely inspired. Under the power of the Holy Spirit, worship unfolds and a sense of hope prevails. The Ghanaian womanist scholar Mercy Amba Oduyoye emphasizes the importance of life-in-community as a continuation of the African world view of kinship cited above: "Africans recognize life as life-in-community. . . . Our nature as beings-in-relationship is a two way relation: with God and with our fellow human beings."[19]

Amid the history of Africans in America claiming their place as unique contributors to the American religious heritage are reminders that there is diversity within the African heritage, which affirms the importance of diversity within African American worship practices.

Furthermore, as denominationalism developed among Black congregations, researchers assume that diversity exists simply in the choices and differences between denominations, thus signaling differences between Black Pentecostals, Baptists, Methodists, Presbyterians, Episcopalians, and so on. The reality is that diversity exits within and among each of the groups identified, according to life lived within the community. Researchers or onlookers are often confused by differences in worship practices, assuming that *all* congregations within the denomination maintained or abandoned the same aspects of African world views based on the denominational choice. Diversity exists as the community, under the guidance of the Spirit, encourages and facilitates the direction.

Not only did diversity exist within denominations, but African American congregations continue into the twenty-first century utilizing their African gifts of "double" or "dual" expressions. Shifts in ritual actions occur through individually led communal expressions, in codewords of songs, and through instrumental accompaniment that alters the momentum, without drawing attention to what is being done.

In the current age of rapidly advancing technology that facilitates the ever-expanding global community, diversity in African American worship continues to expand. Black culture, including elements and characteristics of African American worship, have mingled with and helped to create new worship trends. Within the new and "emerging" forms of worship in America and the world, scholars seek to determine what has resulted from African world views introduced by former slaves and free Africans who have established themselves all over the world. There is no doubt that elements of African American worship exist in gospel music, which is now a global phenomenon, and Spirituals, now included in Protestant and Roman Catholic hymnals, as well as the unique chanting style of gospel hip-hop. Thus, the origin, theological foundations, and early developing stages of African American worship history are vital for the current generation as well as future interpretation by students of worship.

For Discussion

1. Identify four prevailing African world views that undergird a theology of African American worship.

2. What are some problems (dangers) in stereotyping people according to particular styles of worship?

3. How is the African/African American concept of kinship and extended family related to the human family of God?

4. What are the four streams of traditions that inform and shape the content and norms of African American worship?

5. Why is the concept of diversity in African American worship important?

CHAPTER 2

THE AFRICAN RELIGIOUS
HERITAGE

T he majority of Africans who would ultimately shape African American worship came from a 3,000-mile stretch along the west coast of Africa from the Senegal River to the southern limits of Angola. The form and extent of slave trade on the African continent prior to the massive importation of Africans across the Atlantic Ocean indicates the possibility that a small percentage of Africans imported to America might have come from countries other than those along the west coast. Mozambique, the island of Madagascar, East Africa, and southern Sudan were centers of world trade, and it is likely that persons from these areas could have been relocated on the west coast of Africa.[1]

Forms of Communications

Peoples of Africa created a myriad of languages, religions, customs, and political systems, all of which differentiated societies. Although there is no common language—"lingua African"—there are shared fundamental world views that provide a basic system for perceiving and responding to reality that enables African people to make sense out of life situations in order to survive. The family unit and kinship system around which much of life flowed facilitated the establishing of religious belief systems and practices that were integral to life. The deeply engrained urge for expression is represented in art and art forms that evolved as functional adjuncts to African religious rites. The blending of music and rhythmical movement is a universal expression of the interrelatedness of lived experiences. Societal religions were not transmitted through "missionary" efforts. Although religious ideas and customs might have been disseminated

13

through migrations and family linkages, Africans did not bring to America beliefs and practices that would accurately be called monolithic or unified.

Africa—reputedly the location of the Garden of Eden, the birthplace of humanity, and the foundation of civilization—is also noted for its tremendous natural resources. The first 600,000 years of the development of the world's basic survival tools—agriculture, medicine, astrology, the arts, architecture, worship, family life and structure, political systems, states, kingdoms, and empires—took place on this continent. It is no wonder then that this fertile environment, with its skilled and sturdy people, would be the object of ravenous invasions. Ancient Africa, once highly respected, was debased by (European) slave traders over a period of time. The disruption and displacement of its people located Africans in places and positions to help shape the life and culture of people all over the world.[2] In spite of its rich history, the continent was defined as "dark" (in a negative sense) by invaders, who apparently wanted to discredit its significant contributions.

Religious Exposure

Since Africans were among those who helped shape Christian and Islamic religions, it can be assumed that African victims of the world's slave trade were exposed to these religions.[3] Several decades prior to the beginning of the European slave trade, Muslim merchants forcibly transported black Africans across the Sahara desert. It is believed that the first black Africans with whom the (white) Europeans came in actual contact on the coast of West Africa were Muslims of mixed Berber and Arab descent, commonly called "black Moors." Berbers and black Moors were among the Africans captured as slaves by the Portuguese as early as 1440. This may explain why the first Africans in colonial America were often referred to as "Moors" or "Blackamoors." The kingdoms of Ghana, Mali, and Songhay (of ancient western Sudan) had been major Muslim centers.

Islamic influence was apparent during the fifteenth century among the Ghanaians, Mandinka, Fulani, and Hausa. Persons from these societal groups who were subsequently enslaved in the Americas spread Islamic beliefs and practices. There is also evidence that some of the Muslim slaves in the southern colonies in America continued to observe religious customs of Islam.

Christians from Portugal entered the world slave-trading business during the fifteenth century. Under the orders of Prince Henry the Navigator in 1441, traders arrived on the coast of West Africa to investigate the "wealth" reported to be available. Among the "wealth" they found and loaded onto cargo ships were African people, males and females. As a result of this successful venture, the pope conferred upon Prince Henry the title to all the lands to be "discovered" in a specifically defined area along the west coast of Africa. This was the beginning of a new era of systematic exploitation. In the process, some time and energy were expended introducing Christianity along the West African coast.[4] Without even minimal exposure to Christian beliefs, Africans to be imported were baptized by their "pious" captors and then enslaved. African Christians born in Portugal and Spain are reported to have been copartners with European explorers and settlers of America. Like many Europeans, they gained profits from the slave trade.

Christianity was not firmly established along the coastal and inland portions of West Africa until converted Africans, returning from America and Europe, began the evangelization process. There had been earlier evangelization attempts by French and Portuguese Capuchin missionaries during the late fifteenth and early sixteenth centuries. There are records of African converts on the coast of Guinea and in the Congo region dating from this period. Among the converts was an African king, Nzinga Mbemba, who was baptized as Affonso I.[5] Later, many Angolans experienced "conversion" by the Portuguese Church, which took pride in reporting the large number of recent "heathen converts." Accompanied by priests, enslaved Angolans were literally herded to overseas slave-trading departure points and baptized en masse.[6] Because of language barriers, it can be assumed that the mysteries of the faith were never shared with this load of converts. "Dripping wet" from baptism, they crossed the ocean waters to unknown destinations. Baptisms facilitated political and economic, rather than religious, concerns. There was not enough time to translate the tenets of the faith into any of the languages or tongues of the diverse religious cargo scheduled for immediate departure.

Since some of the slaves brought to colonial America came by way of the "Middle Passage," exposure to Christianity might have taken place in the West Indies.[7] According to some accounts, some of the slaves brought to the West Indies after 1517 had been educated as Catholics. A "Negro" in Quivira, Mexico, had actually taken holy orders. Roman Catholics had established three Brotherhoods of the True Cross of Spaniards by 1542, dedicated to the missionizing of Blacks.

Although exposure to Christianity was superficial for some of the slaves, exposure to the beliefs of their captors may have facilitated the Christianization process of Africans in the New World. Many may have discovered that the inconsistency between the Christianity taught and what was practiced could be clarified by imposing their own traditional African beliefs.

Roots of African American Christianity

In spite of the ingrained traditional religious beliefs and customs of the descendants of African American worshipers, colonial Christians generally assumed Africans to be "ignorant heathens." This attitude created an impassable chasm between African and Euro-American worshipers. Reluctant to share a message of love of neighbor and freedom, Euro-Americans shaped and dispensed a more convenient form of Christianity. African recipients were expected to receive the message with its distortions, be "saved," and demonstrate their new Christian state by being "good" slaves.

In such an environment the seeds of African American worship were sown. The slaves' reception of the gospel message and their understanding of worship were not as the colonists presumed they would be. The liberating Word of God freed the slaves to respond in new and creative ways in the midst of their human bondage. A glimpse of this history begins with the shaping of African American communities in colonial America.

African Communities in Colonial America

During the sixteenth century, Holland became the main carrier of captured Africans taken to Spanish America. Because of an accident on one of the slave expeditions, a Dutch ship landed the first group of Africans in the New World.

Among the first twenty Africans, captured and brought to Jamestown, Virginia, in August 1619 were Antoney and Isabella. Like the other eighteen indentured servants, they stepped onto unfamiliar grounds into an unfamiliar social system. They were apparently given unfamiliar non-African names at their hasty baptisms as they were granted the right of entry into the body of Christ. Under British law, which still governed Virginia, baptized servant-slaves could be legally freed when the cause of their enslavement was removed.[8] This first group of Africans in a strange land, equally unfamiliar to their captors, arrived under this law, confident that their freedom would ultimately be granted. It was understood that they would work as servants for a period of time and then be assured of freedom.

Amid the drama of the transporting of millions of Africans, many by way of the West Indies (the "Middle Passage"), and the legalizing of a horrid system of slavery is a record of the marriage of Antoney and Isabella. The birth of their son, William (c. 1623–24), provided two additional "firsts": the first child born in English colonial America of African parentage, and the first baptism of an American-born child of African parentage. This baptism by the Church of England took place at a time when enslaved African peoples looked forward to freedom, just as people of other races had.[9] Little did this pioneering group realize that their position at the Holy Font would soon become a point of political and religious discontent.

According to the first detailed American census of 1624–25, African Americans constituted approximately 2 percent of the total population, all living in Virginia settlements. From 1626 forward, Africans were imported to New Amsterdam on the Hudson River, to Massachusetts, and to other places in the New World, with contracts that would grant them freedom after serving as indentured slaves. Available evidence suggests that many of the first generation of African Americans in Virginia and New York worked out their term of servitude and were freed.[10]

The first African servants arrived in Massachusetts in 1638, where there are records of requested church memberships and marriages.[11] In 1693 a group of slaves in Massachusetts requested permission to form their own separate religious meetings under the guidance of Euro-Americans. According to the earliest recorded account of this endeavor, Cotton Mather responded to their request by aiding them in the shaping of *Rules for the Society of Negroes.* The first rule indicates that a time and form of worship had begun to take shape: "It shall be our Endeavor, to Meet in the Evening after the Sabbath; and Pray together by Turns, one to Begin and another to Conclude the Meeting; And between the two Prayers, A Psalm shall be Sung, and a Sermon Repeated."[12]

These religious "Society" meetings were to take place between 7 and 9 PM, and "no member of the Society should be absent without a reason."

Further evidence of the rigid discipline of members incorporated in the Rules was their concern that all members learn the catechism and be prepared to participate in a catechetical period as one of their usual meeting exercises.[13]

Sociological Context

The general political and religious climate on the east coast of the New World was filled with a variety of problems to be solved. Along with the establishing of new colonies and determining whether they would become involved in slavery were debates about the whole matter of slavery as it had developed.[14]

In 1790 there were 59,557 African Americans who were not slaves, which represented 7.9 percent of the total American population. By 1830, forty years later, the African American population had increased to 13.7 percent. The percentage dropped to 11 percent, with a population of 488,070 in 1860.[15]

In addition to a few free Africans before slavery, indentured servants who had completed their years of service were also part of the "nonslave" or reputedly "free" population.[16] Some slaves were able to obtain their freedom by participating in military service, buying their freedom, or simply by successfully escaping to free territory. Large numbers of free slaves were added through the efforts of abolition and manumission movements. Through territorial expansion where the nonslave was permitted, the incorporation of African Americans in the census count revealed a substantial increase. There remains those unaccounted-for individuals and families who, because of the color of their skin, could phase into the Euro-American community without revealing their African heritage. Some nonslave African Americans owned slaves and apparently did not subject them to the same kind of bondage as Euro-Americans had.

Whereas Euro-Americans took only sporadic notice of early free Africans, the establishing of slave laws made it necessary to distinguish between free and enslaved Africans in subsequent years, especially in the South. It was not unusual for lawmakers to mix free African Americans indiscriminately with slaves because of skin color. During the colonial years, some flexibility allowed free African Americans to vote and hold office. Their free status remained ambiguous because of the color of their skin and ever deepening racist attitudes. Nevertheless, the free status of

African Americans figured strongly in the establishing of free African American churches and congregations, a matter to be considered later.

With an increasing demand for sturdy laborers to prepare crops raised mainly in Southern colonies, African slave trade and subsequently the African population in America increased substantially. Not only did the European and American economists need the slaves' strength and sturdiness, but also the easy availability of slaves made them a source of cheap labor. The dark color of their skin made them highly visible and, therefore, easy to locate if they attempted to escape.

With the increasing African American population through slave importations and the birth of children, social practices and a series of laws relegated Blacks to a marginalized societal position. Although the treatment of slaves was left to the discretion of the colonists, legislation allowed Euro-Americans to impose definitions on a race of people of African origin, both free and enslaved. Vincent Harding suggests that the definitions placed Americans of African descent into three categories: political, economic, and cultural. Although Harding does not make the stipulation, this categorization ultimately and profoundly affected the shaping of African American worship traditions. He contends:

> First, Africans were defined as prisoner-slaves of all Euro-American society and its legal-political structures. Second, as the slaves of individuals, families, and companies, they were often looked upon as semi-animal labor-producing property. Third—a more agonizingly subtle and confused conception—[Africans] were defined as a combination of overgrown and witless children, lost heathen in need of salvation, and fearful, untrustworthy, but fascinating and often desirable sensual savages whose African roots would soon wither away.[17]

By the end of 1630, laws that defined and oppressed African peoples in America also set the tone for a depressive early American Christian ethos. There were laws that denied enslaved African Americans ownership of property, political rights, education, the right to assemble without supervision, and the right to use their own language. In a new world settled initially by persons seeking religious freedom, it was inevitable that legal and religious systems would be closely related. Many rituals connected with African religious practices were declared illegal. Among the practices outlawed in some places were the use of drums and dancing or excessive physical movement, and the rite of passage at death—funerals. Euro-American fear of the unfamiliar and the need to be in control apparently caused the declaration of certain worship practices as "heathen" and "paganistic." This negative labeling was also an attempt to sever African historical roots. The elimination of history and nurturing roots forces people into a state of dependency, which makes enslavement much more manageable.

Legislation that granted tacit approval of the institution of slavery occurred in the same year of the earliest recorded evidence of an adult slave baptism: 1641. Hidden (perhaps appropriately) by the Massachusetts "Body of Liberties Laws" is documentation of the reception and baptism of an African slave woman into a church in Dorchester, Massachusetts.[18] Paradoxically, as the human rights and mobility of Africans in America were legally curtailed, a "legal" right of entry into the body of Christ was granted. This religious passage also sanctioned lifetime subjugation by a supposedly loving faith community. Without sufficient evidence to the contrary, we can assume that there was about as much love and nurture surrounding baptisms as there was in the room where slave laws were hammered out! Economic, rather than sincere, faith motives had quickly become the criteria for providing religious instruction and baptism of slaves.

The Anglican Church apparently baptized and admitted slaves regularly during the seventeenth century. In the year of the first recorded adult baptism (1641), there were at least forty "African" members on the roll of Bouweire Chapel in New Amsterdam.[19] In spite of this documentation, religious instruction and baptism of slaves were not top priority for the Euro-Americans. In addition to their fear that baptism would then require the freeing of slaves, the early settlers were mainly concerned about their own economic survival and physical safety. The missionary-minded among them often complained that slaveholders would not allow slaves to be catechized because of their fear that they would lose some of their slave-force after the slave was baptized. In spite of the Christian commission to "preach the gospel to all nations," baptism and subsequent freedom of the slaves interfered with colonial economic interest. In order to maintain the tenets of the faith, there was much discussion on this matter with the conclusion that it was their Christian duty to "cleanse and whiten the souls of heathens."

Laws as early as 1664 relegated African slaves to perpetual bondage—*durante vita*. Virginia was first to enact a law that stated, in essence, that the conferring of baptism would not alter the condition of the person as to her or his bondage or freedom. By 1706, six colonies had legislated that baptism was not a threat to a slaveholder's legal rights.[20]

Some of the concerns were not limited to those who held slaves in bondage. Francis Le Jau, a missionary in Goose Creek, South Carolina, provided the following declaration to which adult slave candidates for baptism were required to assent or subject themselves before they were baptized:

> You declare in the presence of God and before this Congregation that you do not ask for the holy baptism out of any design to free yourself from the Duty and Obedience that you owe to your Master while you live, but merely for the good of your Soul and to partake of the Graces and Blessings promised to the members of the Church of Jesus Christ.[21]

The separation of baptism and liberation apparently freed the African American convert to recognize the systemic hypocrisy of Euro-Americans who claimed to be Christian. As a result, some slaves avoided evangelization. Those who did receive religious instruction gained facility in adjusting to superficial freedom: (1) freedom in Christ, (2) freedom from human bondage, and (3) freedom to interact with other Christians. Numerous slave narratives refer to the obvious inconsistencies of slaveholders who in essence talked the liberty of the gospel and lived as if they did not believe what they had said.

The discomfort and unhappiness created and deepened an urgency for slaves to listen to God directly for directions for empowerment. In numerous secret gatherings, some heard rebellion; some heard physical escape by running away; and others heard patience in the process of "using the system." Some converted slaves "honored" their conversion and baptism while remaining bonded servants. At the risk of being chided by other slaves, some sought religious instruction and baptism as a potential "ticket to freedom" for themselves and others. Religious instruction was not limited to what was provided by Euro-American missionizers. Persons within the African American community were appointed by slaveholders or were self-appointed to teach. Le Jau provides evidence of baptized slaves who could be trusted to instruct one another and who were zealous and honest in relationships with their "peers" and the slaveholders.

Judicial legislation accommodated slaveholders on matters of time for religious instruction and the treatment of slaves. There was concern that evangelization, conversion, and baptism would actually ruin the slaves and make them proud, saucy, ungovernable, and especially rebellious.[22] During the first century and a half of slavery, through the efforts of the

Society for the Propagation of the Gospel in Foreign Parts (SPG) from 1702 to 1785, a small number of slaves were able to receive religious instructions. Some of the factors that prevented greater exposure were the objection of slaveholders, especially in Southern colonies; scarcity of catechizers; barriers of culture and language; and the time involved, which would take slaves away from their work.

The mobility and worship involvement varied from one slave community to another. Whereas some slaves were forbidden to attend worship services in some communities, others were forced to attend or were granted worship privileges. It was not unusual for slave attendance to exceed the number of Euro-Americans at racially mixed worship. A sincere Christian fellowship seldom existed between slave members and their Euro-American brothers and sisters in daily life or in worship. The Table meal, or Lord's Supper, was one obvious division of the body of Christ. Predetermined seating arrangements relegated slaves to balconies, back rows, spaces outside the church building, near back windows, or wherever the persons "in charge" indicated. To truly isolate slaves, churches are known to have dug pits just below the pulpit for the crowding-in of Black worshipers.[23]

African Spirituality

The theme that has permeated the first two chapters of this book is the importance of an *African Spirituality*, the sacred cosmos that helped African people survive in America and throughout the African Diaspora. The basic premise of African Spirituality is the interrelatedness of all of life, beginning with the creation of all there is by a divine Creator—called by different names but understood as Uniquely One, and extending to the smallest existing form of life. Life for African people who continue to adhere to African Traditional Religions (ATR) is viewed and lived holistically. Internalizing and living such a view of life allows humans to understand and believe that God, the Creator, remains present and is dynamically involved in the world. The cosmos, the entire universe, is sacred, and all that God has made is not only sacred, but divinely linked. Cosmic "rhythm" is the embodiment of divine order, providing the basis for life together, and the means by which life pulsates.

Continuing in the African tradition, it is not surprising to find the Egyptian idea of nature as "netcher" or "neter," also the synonym for God

as corporeal manifestation of all physical reality. A "netcher" is not God, per se; it is instead an integral part of that who God is.[24] Among the Egyptians, *spirit* is translated *kha ba*, meaning "holy breath," and was later developed by the Hebrews as *ruach* (Spirit), and by the Greeks as *pneuma* (Spirit). Nature and spirit, Creator and Creation are viewed as a unified reality in African cosmology, thus providing an important foundation for African Spirituality. It is the freedom of God to be God, to continually create and transform reality, that gave hope to African slaves as they struggled to make sense of a life of forced oppression and dehumanization.

As Africans in the American Diaspora were able to hear and find meaning in biblical concepts, they were able to build upon the African Spirituality that they had internalized and transmitted orally in order to survive the horrors of the American scene. By now as African Americans they could steal away and establish their own form of Christianity.

For Discussion

1. What is likely to happen if the historical roots of a people are eroded (uprooted)?

2. What historical evidence is there for the exposure of Africans to Christianity prior to the era of American slave trade?

3. In what ways does your denominational polity free communities of faith to worship in spirit and in truth, utilizing cultural traditions of local congregations? In what ways does the polity limit freedom?

4. African Spirituality is reflected in the freedom to improvise in worship. How can this be explained?

5. As you seek further clarity about the African worship heritage, invite some Africans from your community to dialogue with a study group from your congregation about worship (both traditional and Christian African) in their particular culture. Plan a worship service together that, with integrity, will provide practices reflective of the African traditions as well as traditions represented in the study group.

CHAPTER 3

WORSHIP IN THE INVISIBLE INSTITUTION

Aplethora of testimonies of freed and fugitive slaves indicates that Christian worship experiences were not limited to the visible worshiping places of Euro-Americans. Slaves developed a worship life of their own in secret places at times determined by the slave community. Although risky, such secrecy transcended the daunting eyes and ears of slaveholders and overseers. In search of the truth of the gospel, slaves established ways to express their faith in worship and in their daily lives commensurate to their understanding of the biblical message. Secluded in "brush arbors" (also identified as "bush" or "hush arbors"), slave cabins, woods, deep gullies or ravines, swamps, or simply in "the bottoms," slaves transformed the Americanized version of Christianity into a form with which they could identify. This was most often done by grafting "Christian ideas onto traditional African roots."[1] This secret worship life of the slaves later became known as the "Invisible Institution." The label provides an affirmation of the clandestine or "invisible" nature of events where mutual relationships, world views, behavior patterns, and social and political actions were "officially constituted" by the slaves. Gatherings of the "Invisible Institution" occurred with such frequency that they are considered foundational to the subsequent establishment of African American "visible institutions": congregations, denominations, schools, burial associations, fraternal orders, sororities, political movements, and organizations for the pursuit of justice and equality.

Scattered throughout extant writings, testimonies, and oral records of ex-slaves from this period are helpful data concerning the worship of this unique institution. Some of the key characteristics consistent in these accounts are:

—the importance of private, divine space where freedom could be sought and experienced;

—ownership of a Christian belief system and code of religion that they could call their own;

—the uncomplicated manner of worship, conducted in the way of the folks, without outside interference;

—the divinely inspired, minimally educated but biblically artic-ulate preachers, called from among the plantation folks, with a sensitivity to the plight of the folks;

—freedom of the Spirit to enable the preaching, singing, praying, shouting, and responsive listening of the Spirit-filled congregations;

—freedom to worship at a time that slaves would determine for themselves;

—mutual community affinity where "everybody's heart was in tune, so when they called on God, they made heaven ring"; and

—with the support of the community, slaves could experience and be sustained with new life and move with hope into the future.[2]

In secret gatherings, African descendants risked their lives as they honed and expressed their own beliefs in response to Almighty God. Exposure to the New World environment, New World Christianity, and newly arriving Africans allowed them to contextualize Christianity while being reminded of traditional African religions. Over the period of time from the arrival of Africans in Virginia in 1619, new verbal language forms had evolved. In the process, however, basic symbols, symbolism, and manners of expression used in traditional African communication had been retained. Exposed to new ways of life and means of livelihood, they had been made aware of the meaning of marginalization, oppression, and degradation, all of which affected their psyches. In an effort to find freedom and understanding, traditional beliefs and practices, Christian beliefs and practices, and the reality of existence merged. As a result, a unique African American Christian faith was shaped. The biblical mes-sage of salvation assured deliverance from oppression and hope for the future. The biblical Jesus, whose earthly existence was similar to their own, was clearly the Liberator. He, too, was despised, mistreated, and ulti-mately lynched. His defeat of all earthly oppression, assured in his resurrection, ascension, and promise of peace, was the foundation of hope for the slave.

Sacred Space

Former slaves recalled the use of quilts and blankets saturated with water, hung so that sacred space (a sanctuary) was defined for worshipers to gather. This improvised "architecture," equipped with a large black iron wash pot full of water in the center of the space, would deaden the sound so that their voices could not easily be heard outside the immediate space. A person preaching or leading prayer would lean over and speak directly into the water-filled pot so that the sound could be "drowned." Another procedure used to "catch" the sound was to invert an iron pot and prop it up with a rock or large stick. The sound could also be caught or focused in the sacred space by suspending the large pot upside down from one or more large tree limbs. The community of faith would also sing as softly as possible with their heads huddled together around the inverted or water-filled pot.

There is yet another theory that the inverted pots served an important symbolic function. Albert J. Raboteau cites the words of a former slave in Tennessee who claimed that "dere ole iron cookin' pots [turned] upside down on de groun' neah dere cabins . . . showed dat Gawd waz wid dem."[3] The symbolic presence of God in their midst harkens back to religious practices in Africa, where symbols of the presence of God were important. Another speculation is that an inverted pot is a representation of one of the symbols of the Yoruba god Eshu Elegba. There are also ceremonies in the Caribbean where large vessels are used simply to hold water and sacred objects during religious ceremonies. Some of the slaves might have recalled this practice during their middle passage.

I recently observed the use of a large pot at the center of an informal worship service in one rural section of West Africa. Although contradicting reasons were given for the presence of the pot, there was a consensus that it had always been part of the tradition. This supports the theory that this custom might be of African origin. The original purpose of the pot in Africa requires speculation since there is no definitive data on an origin that would extend its purpose into a new world. Nevertheless, for the enslaved African American the black iron pot apparently served a useful purpose throughout the active period of the Invisible Institution.

Praise and Fellowship

The festive dimension of slave worship was enhanced and encouraged when permission was granted by some slaveholders for separate worship services. Christian slaves from local and neighboring plantations were able to "have a good time in the Lord" before, during, and after worship. During camp meetings, slaves from surrounding plantations were allowed to attend, which provided another opportunity for fellowship and excitement. Many slaves who did not profess Christianity would attend camp meeting services for the purpose of socializing and participating in the festive moments of religious freedom. After service, slaves often continued their own form of camp meeting worship in secrecy, after the closing benediction, well into the wee hours of the morning. Here in the Invisible Institution, away from the questioning eyes of the slaveholders, slaves could freely express themselves in the presence of One who cared about their humanity. In secrecy, the songs heard and sung earlier in camp meeting settings would be remembered and reworked. A sermon would be preached in "storytelling fashion," utilizing rhythmical tones and musical cadences that were appealing and that met the needs of the slaves. The response of the people could then be commensurate with the timbre and style of a people who, although oppressed, could participate wholeheartedly.

Elements of Worship in the Invisible Institution

Elements (components, or essential acts) of worship can be determined from the oral transmission of practices, documentation in slave narratives, diaries, letters, and writings of observers. Although freedom, spontaneity, and emotionalism in slave worship are often highlighted, there is also evidence of "liturgical form" and a sense of a rhythmic flow of the service. Within the much sought-after freedom in worship was an apparent development of some semblance of order, although it could not be categorized as "strict order." Worship was truly *leitourgia*, the work of a particular people.

In the light of the clandestine nature of worship in the Invisible Institution, it can be assumed that all identifiable elements may *not* have been included in all services. The manner and style of the execution of elements are perhaps as important as what was done. One of the most distinguishing characteristics of worship is the (often) inseparability of distinct elements. Music, movement, and song were apparently constant dynamics, providing the foundation upon which all elements were carried out. For instance, the musical quality of the preaching and praying would indicate that much of the worship was sung liturgy. Similar dynamics existed during the "call and response" dialogue between the preacher and the congregation. The momentum of the total service was precipitated by Spirit-filled encounters with God—both corporate and personal—combined with spiritual and emotional needs of the gathered community.

The basic elements of worship included praying, singing, preaching of the Word, shouting, and communal fellowship. There is also evidence of calls to worship, community concerns, conversion, testimonies, and confessions of sins in many gatherings. Each of these will be briefly explored.

Call to Worship

Since worship was to take place in secrecy, worship was "called" or announced long before the community assembled. There was generally an understanding among the slaves as to the time and place of "the meeting," which was confirmed in song as the slaves went about their work. Slave songs (Spirituals) such as "Steal Away," "(Get You Ready) There's a Meeting Here Tonight," and "Over My Head" are identified in slave narratives as songs that announced "calls to religious meeting." Wash Wilson, a former slave, described his own experience in the Invisible Institution: "Steal away to Jesus . . . mean dere gwine be a 'ligious meetin' dat night. De masters . . . didn't like dem . . . meetin's, so ous natcherly slips off at night, down in the bottoms or somewhere. Sometimes us sing and pray all night."[4]

A number of code words and symbolic actions were used to identify the place of worship. The breaking of tree limbs so that they pointed in the direction of the appointed place was one way of directing worshipers to the exact place. The time of worship was not determined by humanly constructed clocks. Perhaps in keeping with the African concept of time and by virtue of the fact that for the slave time revolved around the work schedule of someone else and was therefore irrelevant, the correct starting time was whenever two or three were gathered in the name of Jesus.

With or without a preacher, a part of the call included a time of corporate support and reconnecting with the community. A vivid description of this reentry time is given by a former slave: "They first ask each other how they feel, the state of their minds, and so forth. . . . The slaves forget all their suffering, except to remind others of the trials during the past week, exclaiming: 'Thank God, I shall not live here always!'"[5]

The gathering community greeted and welcomed one another, shaking hands, embracing, and offering expressions of joy as worship began.

Praying (Prayer)

A continuation of the African religious heritage is clearly evident in the forms and frequency of prayers, as well as in an understanding that prayer is the heart of worship.[6] This was especially true during secret gatherings of African Americans. Prayer was for the early worshipers, and remains today, "the most important way to remain in communication with Almighty God who, though in constant communion with them, could be reached in privacy."[7] As slaves gradually became acquainted with biblical concepts, the continuity of traditional African religious beliefs and practices provided a firm foundation upon which their faith would grow. The desire for freedom, which could come only from God, was a constant theme of prayers. Exhausted from their daily labors, worshipers, in secret environments of the Invisible Institution, often found physical and mental relief in prayer. Prayers were often spontaneous, occurring frequently in the service, and always improvised in the light of existential personal and community needs and hopes.

Prayer time, which occurred frequently, provided additional impetus for communal participation. The current African American prayer tradition, shaped during this early period of worship history, has been identified as a "prayer event."[8] Rather than passively listening to a prayer, the gathered community becomes involved with the prayer leader, using a variety of responses. There might be verbal "witnessing" to what is being prayed, such as "Amen!"; "Thank you, Jesus!"; or "Yes, Lord!" There might be direct urging or nudging of the leader to "Pray your prayer!" or "Tell it to the Lord!" There are often injections of admonitions to God to "Come by here"; "Oh, help him, Jesus"; "Hear us . . ."; or "Help us now, Lord!" Some participants moan or hum in perfect cadence with the prayer leader. Some rock, sway, cry softly, or merely nod their heads in assent. The "prayer event" often reaches full intensity as the leader and congregation, filled with the Spirit, demonstrate that everyone's heart is spiritually "in tune."

In keeping with their African traditions, the prayers of early African American worshipers included invocations, adoration, praise, thanksgiving, intercession, and petition. Prayers after sermons would often drive home the message of the sermon or exhort the congregation on the basis of personal experience with God. Harold Carter notes the carryover of this tradition in the prayer of a woman in a twentieth-century revival meeting who, with "the robe of prayer," was equipped as "one to speak with drive and authority to the community." Convinced during the sermon that she was included in God's elect, she gained strength to challenge others in her prayer to "receive what she had experienced by being convicted and converted."[9]

Freedom, liberation, and deliverance were naturally the major themes of prayers. Slaves prayed for the day when they would be free from cares of "this old mean world." This was not an "otherworld-after-death" concern as much as it was for immediate freedom in this world, even in the North, by way of the underground railroad or other means of escape. They had an unusual gift for incorporating the present situation, with their memories of freedom in Africa, and the Old Testament exodus of the Hebrews from slavery. They identified also with the situations of Daniel in the lions' den and Shadrach, Meshach, and Abednego in the fiery furnace, and they prayed for the day when God would likewise step in and save them.

Prayer for slaves and slaveholders provided an effective means and symbol of resistance. Slaveholders who also believed in the power of prayer found the praying of slaves meaningful and effective. Slaves were often asked by slaveholders to pray for some of the immediate concerns of the oppressor. Openly, their responses and prayers were in keeping with the requests. In the invisible institutions, these prayers were occasionally altered to incorporate the slaves' own concerns as well. In both instances the prayer included the phrase "the Lord's will be done," indicating the slaves' reliance upon God to know what was best.

Singing

The response to God in song, also rooted in traditional African religions, was and is another way worshipers are enabled to engage their total beings in prayer. Evidence of the linkage of prayer and song is cited by Anderson Edwards, an ex-slave:

31

We prayed a lot to be free and the Lord done heered us. We didn't have no song books and the Lord done give us our songs and when we sing them at night it jus' whispering so nobody hear us. One went like this:

> "My knee bones am aching,
> My body's rackin' with pain,
> I 'lieve I'm a chile of God,
> And this ain't my home,
> 'Cause Heaven's my aim."[10]

The extraordinary gifts of singing and creating new songs have been widely acclaimed.[11] Singing as an inseparable part of life is convincingly attested to by slaves in narratives and in the texts of songs that they shaped and transmitted. One did not stop whatever else one was doing to sing. Songs could enhance the moment, or for particular situations they simply flowed forth from a song leader and connected with the spirit of others who joined in the singing. The sound of the singing and the words of songs have been described as wild, weird, plaintive, sad, and sorrowful by observers. W. E. B. DuBois' often-quoted reference to slave songs as "sorrow songs" prepared the foundation for additional serious study of Spirituals. His observation that these songs are the most beautiful expression of human experience born on this side of the seas gets at the affirmation of life and hope of slave singers.[12] The frequently employed "call and response" form, inherited from African tradition, facilitated the hearing and learning of texts and helped ensure a bonded community.

In music and song, Africans in America were lifted closer to God and to one another as they struggled to bear the conditions of their forced situations. Singing is an artistic form inextricably interwoven into the fabric of all African cultures. It provides a divine channel through which God speaks and believers respond. As I have said elsewhere:

> For an African people, music is not merely a means of expressing feel-
> ings. It [music] evokes the reciprocal activity of imagination and under-
> standing of the soul. Since the Soul is the center of God's human work,
> only the believer's love of God allows the soul to respond through and
> in music. Thus in anticipation of W. E. B. DuBois' statement, "music is
> the soul of Black Folks," the sound of music born of human breath bore
> witness to the presence and love of God in the being of Black folks from
> the beginning of time.[13]

As for their African forebears, the singing of the community at work and worship connected the sacred-secular dimensions of life. In improvised texts, melodies, harmonies, and rhythms, slaves shaped a distinct African American theology out of their own understanding of Scripture. Embodied in this new theology was an affirmation of life and belief that "God is always on time." The religious folk songs (or slave songs, which were later called Spirituals) are also documentations of God's divine intervention in human history, which affected both the oppressed and the oppressors.

The intentions of worshipers and some of the worship practices are reflected in slave songs, most notably the following:

> I sought my Lord in de wilderness,
> In de wilderness, in de wilderness;
> I sought my Lord in the wilderness,
> For I'm a-going home.
> As I went down to de valley to pray,
> Studying about dat good old way,
> When you shall wear de starry crown,
> Good Lord, show me de way.
> O mourner, let's go down,
> Let's go down, let's go down
> O mourner, let's go down,
> Down, in de valley to pray.

Slave songs served a dual purpose. Through songs, at worship or at work, slaves could also communicate with one another. Many songs, couched in religious language, not only expressed the faith of the people, but also provided signals for the time and place of the next "underground railroad train," which could lead them out of human bondage into freedom.

Singing has a mysterious power that frees the human spirit so that the Spirit of God can penetrate and, in the words of James Cone, also "intensify the power of the Spirit's presence with the people."[14] Slaves understood clearly that the Holy Spirit is free to move at will and cannot be manipulated. Singing, whether as prayer or as a response to prayers and other elements of worship, helped create a mood of freedom, an openness to quicken an awareness of God's presence, and for the hearing and receiving of God's grace.

Preaching

The Word of God heard and experienced in a free worshiping environment was the foundation for secret meetings of the Invisible Institution. Though not articulated in carefully worded formulas or creeds, the Word preached was clearly incarnate in Jesus. From texts of Spirituals and extant sermons, we learn that expressions about God were not always theologically different from statements about Jesus. The slaves perceived God as Father, Son, and Holy Spirit, especially in the slave Spirituals, as an indivisible unity. The first and last (alpha and omega), King of kings, Lord of lords, was Jesus the Christ, and "no [one] works like him." In thoughts of physical death, preachers and singers would say: "When I Come to Die, Give Me Jesus!" Cone contends that "for black slaves, Jesus is God, breaking [himself] into [our] historical presence and transforming it according to divine expectations."[15]

> Jesus, then, was not thought of in their heads to be analyzed in relation to a related thought called "God." Jesus was an experience, a historical presence in motion, liberating and moving the people in freedom.[16]

The reality of Jesus, Emmanuel (God with us) allowed a "hands-on" experience with God in the flesh for slaves. To meet God is to encounter Jesus, both divine and human, immanent and transcendent. The biblical facts that Jesus was born of a (human) woman, that he identified with the poor and suffering, conquered death, and now lives again were sufficient proof that God cared about them and would set them free. Jesus' life among the common people, his pain, suffering, agony, and ultimate death on the "tree" at the hands of cruel people made him a reality. The slaves, too, were experiencing the harshness of life, but could look with hope into a future with the Almighty. Worship in privacy girded them with a divine "Jesus armour," which strengthened them to "walk together and not get weary."[17]

The time of preaching in worship enabled slaves to hear and experience the Word, good news of liberation, salvation and sanctification. This necessitated a person, divinely inspired, called by God, and affirmed by the community, who could stand in the divine place (at the improvised pulpit) and deliver the Word. Also required was some knowledge of the Bible, combined with the ability to speak and communicate this sacred knowledge. The preacher, therefore, played an important role as mediator/priest and especially prophet. Slaves were no doubt familiar with comparable roles from the African heritage. As mediator/priest, the preacher functioned as "the voice from God," *a griot*.[18] She or he was a specialist in divine matters and could be called upon to perform certain rites and rituals on behalf of the people. Just as in Africa, the mediator/priest was a religious symbol among the people whose encounter with God had been "recognized" and accepted by the people. They were also given authority by the religious community to serve as leader, priest and pastor, and prophet for the community.[19]

The roles of priest as leader, diviner, seer, and medium are also rooted in African traditions. Whereas prophets may have other religious or political functions in their African societies, there were none who claimed to be the prophetic mouthpiece of the Supreme God, in the manner similar to biblical prophets.[20] In a new Christian environment, African American "prophets" combined the African and Judeo-Christian roles as charismatic leaders called of God to hear and then make forthright pronouncements as divine proclaimers. Invisible Institutions, and later free churches, were greatly influenced by prophetic preachers "who would use their spiritual powers and charisma to struggle against oppression and for liberation."[21] The timeless Word of God is to be heard by people in every age and context, so that the prophetic role of the preacher is to relate the biblical message to life and life situations.

Whereas not all slave preachers were revolutionary prophets like Nat Turner, who called the people to action, such prophets did emerge from time to time. Preachers on the whole apparently discouraged violent reactions or revolts. In spite of this, their potential to become revolutionaries often caused them to be judged by slaveholders as dangerous to society. Later in the rural South, when "praise houses" (see chap. 4) more or less supplemented or replaced the Invisible Institution and after several attempted insurrections, there was a general concern among slave owners that "there should be more praying and less preaching, for preaching breeds faction, but praying causes devotion."[22]

A prophetic voice could be heard each time a slave preacher would assert that "God tol' me that freedom was right down the road; we's got to be patient" and "we will all receive forty acres and a mule." The prophetic voice was calling the community to keep the faith. Eugene D. Genovese rightfully observed that "the joyous cries of Jubilee-Jubilo came down with overwhelming frequency to refer to distinct and realistic goals, not to a transition to the Christian Paradise."[23]

Sermons of slave preachers reminded the people that the deliverer had already come in Jesus the Christ, who dwelled in their midst and could be called upon by faith. Their prophetic role as preacher was to listen to the Word and help the congregation "claim the news." Their prophecies encouraged believers to look with faith to deliverance from their bondage without falling into a state of "otherworldly passivity."[24] What appeared to outsiders as passive joy and happiness in their contemporary (slave) state was instead the African world view "strategy of patience" and a means of survival. The emotional fervor that was characteristically part of the response of the people upon experiencing the good news of God's Word was cathartic, yes, but also a means of survival.

Shouting

Clarity must be given at the outset about two basic forms of shouting: "Regular" shouting of individuals (which will be referred to simply as "shouting") and the "ring shout," a ritualized, group activity clearly of African origin, which gained momentum in "praise houses." The ring shout will be discussed in chapter 4, "Praise House Worship."

Shouting is experienced when the Holy Spirit fills and empowers the worshipers so that they are unable to remain still. Shouting is one way that a person responds to the encounter and movement of the Holy Spirit in worship. The resulting physical involvement has been described as religious ecstasy, or uncontrollable physical movements involving one's whole person. The shouters may stand and dance or jump about involuntarily, or they may remain seated and swing their arms and legs convulsively. African Americans understand this as a special divine moment of happiness and joy during a spontaneous encounter with and enabling of the Holy Spirit. This ecstatic moment may be referred to as "getting happy." What happens to cause one to shout must also be understood in the context of one's psychological and religious orientation, needs, and expectations, as well as the accompanying element(s) of worship (preaching, praying, singing, or the shouting) of someone else.

The Invisible Institution was not an accident of a few rebellious people. It was a divine necessity for a people for whom religion was integrally related to all of life. The hypocrisy of a distorted gospel, heard under the influence of slave masters who desired to keep slaves in check, forced the slaves to identify time and space where they could freely be in communion with God and with one another. Hearing the words from the Bible interpreted in the light of their oppressed condition freed the slave worshipers to pour out their sufferings and needs and express their joys in their own sacred space. Separate and apart from those who denied them freedom on earth, slaves were free in worship to hear and respond to the Word of God. They could hear and recall the message of salvation and deliverance and increase their faith in God, whose Son, Jesus, had overcome earthly suffering. They could find mental and emotional release in spite of their physical enslavement. They could experience the freedom of verbal and nonverbal expression. They could give and receive affirmation, support, and encouragement. They could worship God with their whole being. They dared to risk the punishment they would surely receive if their Invisible Institution became visible to the slave masters.

For Discussion

1. What are similarities between the African American "Invisible Institution" and early Judeo-Christian worship? What are some differences?

2. In the light of their imposed slave status, how do you suppose slaves viewed the servant role Jesus assumed for himself? What evidence is documented in some of the Spirituals to support your thesis?

3. What is your perception of ways that the preacher in your worship experience relates the biblical message to life situations? Are these related to current local and global events?

4. Invite a group to engage in a simulation of secret worship. From whom would this group be hiding and for what reasons?

CHAPTER 4

PRAISE HOUSE WORSHIP

Praise houses (also referred to as "Pray's Houses," "Prayer Houses," "Pray Houses," or "de place way oner go fur pray") originated on the Sea Islands, off the coasts of South Carolina and Georgia. On the Sea Islands in 1861, 83 percent of the population was of African origin (approx. 11,000). For generations these people of African descent had been isolated and were, therefore, able to preserve African and newly shaping African American practices longer than in other places. During slavery, praise houses were "acceptable" places for slaves to hold religious "meetings." For this reason, praise houses could technically be called the first "visible" institutions or worship spaces in which African American worship traditions were developed.

Initially, praise house worship space was provided and supervised by slaveholders. Euro-American pastors or someone designated by the plantation owners would "oversee" the proceedings. Later, when the religious development of slaves was approved (for whatever reason) or the planters became more lenient, slaves would hold midweek and Sunday evening services under the supervision and leadership of an African American preacher. Services would be held in cabins, barns, cotton houses, or in small, one-room buildings, intentionally constructed as "praise houses."

With or without an appointed supervisor or a preacher, the praise house was a place for special religious celebrations. Unlike the required secrecy of Invisible Institutions, slaves in praise houses had the freedom to sing, pray, shout, read Scriptures, exhort, and experience conversion. The exhorter was always one whose knowledge of the Bible met the approval of the people.

A song leader who knew hymns and psalms from memory was almost as important as the exhorter. The slaves, led by a male or female song leader, sang metered hymns as slowly as the American religious colonists had sung psalms a century earlier. In praise houses, this form of psalm singing began to assume a different, "blackenized" musical shape. Other practices of the earlier "praise house" days are similar to the praise houses still in existence.

The "praise house" tradition of African American worship can be experienced currently in a few communities along the coast of South Carolina. The crude, wood buildings are reminiscent of the descriptions given by ex-slaves and writers of the nineteenth century. Attendance at services held once a month has fallen off, according to one elderly worshiper. However, the enthusiasm engendered after a "warming-up" period is highly contagious. Early in the service one is made aware of the percussive sound produced by the rhythmic tapping of feet on the wood plank floor during the periods of song and prayer. Tapping of feet also follows testimonies, or to indicate approval when the congregation is pleased with someone's comments. Unusual and difficult syncopated forms of handclapping occur during the singing, which seems to be familiar to regular worshipers. Visitors are carefully nudged when their rhythm is not in keeping with what is currently taking place.

The leader for the service is either male or female and is most often referred to by the traditional title "foreman." This person serves as facilitator rather than dictator, skillfully guiding the proceedings and encouraging the involvement of the entire gathered community. Although acts of worship are spontaneous, the songs chosen generally alternate between fast and slow tempos, providing a balance in the flow of the service. Prayers, testimonies, and commentaries are evenly spaced between the corporate singing of the community and the reading or reciting of Scripture, indicating a rather carefully planned ordering of elements.

A preacher, a lay speaker, or one gifted as an exhorter delivers a brief exhortation (or "'hortashun") at a point in the service when the people seem "open and ready." Slow, metered hymns are "lined out" by a song leader, with the congregation surging in before the line being delivered has ended. This style of singing "metered hymns," also called "Dr. Watts," continues especially among African American Baptists and some Methodist congregations in the rural South. The dominant language of the service in the praise house is Gullah, a merger of languages and dialects spoken along the west coast of Africa and the English language dialect of planters in the southern part of the United States. This necessitates attentive listening by visitors and by any who are not familiar with the Gullah language in order to keep abreast of what is being said, prayed, or sung.

Ring Shout

The ring shout is frequently described as a practice in praise houses in rural southeastern states, especially South Carolina. It can best be described as a ritualized group activity, clearly of African origin, that could last up to five hours. Children as well as adults participated enthusiastically in ring shouts.

One of the earliest accounts of dancing in worship is a description given by John F. Watson as he expressed outrage over some of the religious practices among Methodists. Watson contends that some of the practices of African Americans had affected the religious manners of some whites. He includes the following description, which was apparently a "most exceptionable error" being tolerated:

> In the blacks' quarter, the coloured people get together, and sing for hours together, short scraps of disjointed affirmations, pledges, or prayers. . . . These are all sung in the merry chorus-manner of the southern harvest field, or husking-frolic method of the slave blacks; and also very like the Indian dances. With every word so sung, they have a sinking of one or other leg of the body alternately; producing an audible sound of the feet at every step, and as manifest as the steps of actual dancing in Virginia.[1]

Whether this was an actual ring shout is debatable, since later descriptions indicate that the feet of shouters are hardly lifted from the floor. Among the many descriptions from the nineteenth century is that of William Francis Allen, Charles Pickard Ware, and Lucy McKim Garrison. Although lengthy, this full description contextualizes characteristics of the dance and "rules" for dancers, including "shuffling" rather than lifting feet off the floor.

> The true "shout" takes place on Sundays or on "praise"-nights through the week, and either in the praise-house or in some cabin in which a regular religious meeting has been held. Very likely more than half the population of the plantation is gathered together. . . . The benches are pushed back to the wall when the formal meeting is over, and old and young, women and men . . . boys with tattered shirts and men's trousers, young girls barefooted, all stand up in the middle of the floor, and when the "sperichl" (Spiritual) is struck up, begin first walking and by-and-by shuffling round, one after the other, in a ring. The foot is hardly taken from the floor, and the progression is mainly due to a jerking, hitching motion, which agitates the entire shouter; and soon brings out streams

of perspiration. Sometimes they dance silently, sometimes as they shuffle they sing the chorus of the spiritual, and sometimes the song itself is also sung by the dancers. But more frequently a band, composed of some of the best singers and of tired shouters, stand at the side of the room to "base" the others, singing the body of the song, and clapping their hands together or on the knees. Song and dance are alike extremely energetic, and often, when the shout lasts into the middle of the night, the monotonous thud, thud of the feet prevents sleep within a half mile of the praise-house.[2]

Although there are no references to this form of shouting in secrecy, we can assume that it might have occurred. The fact that this African ritual did not die before praise houses were acceptable places for religious meetings might be attributed to the flow of new arrivals from Africa and the strong influence of African cultures on the coasts of South Carolina.

Euro-American planters attempted to discourage ring shouts, considering the practice barbaric, senseless, and without biblical warrant. Unaware of, or with little or no appreciation for, African cultures, they could not understand the African propensity for the inseparability of music, prayer, and movement as means of communication with God. They were also apparently not aware of the freedom of the Holy Spirit to take possession of a person's soul and body at the peak experience of worship. Nevertheless, the practice persisted, with traces remaining today.

Although some observers perceived the ring shout as a form of secular dancing, shouters worked diligently to maintain the sacred emphasis. Since regular dancing for the converted was prohibited by the evangelizers, care was taken to distinguish their Spirit-filled inspiration and cathartic longings from mere worldly dancing. One way to do this was to refrain from lifting the feet from the floor or crossing one foot over the other as would happen in regular dancing. With shoulders close together, shouters swayed their bodies and shuffled around in a circle (or "ring," the source of the name). The movement began slowly at first, with a gradual increase of tempo, eventually displaying signs of a frenzy as the song assumed the style of a wild, monotonous chant.

Ring shouts were not limited to praise houses in the South, nor to any one denomination. African American soldiers transported the ring shout to Civil War army camps.[3] Remnants of the ring shouts were also reported in Virginia, Alabama, Florida, and Georgia. James Weldon Johnson reported that he had witnessed shouts at camp meetings, revivals, and at the end of worship in organized churches. Richard Allen, founder of the African Methodist Church, was highly critical of African carryovers in Christian worship, including the ring shout. Daniel Payne, bishop of the African Methodist Episcopal Church, equally critical of the "heathenist" ways of worshipers, attempted to discourage its use to the point of excommunicating members who were found participating. In response to pastors who questioned his motives, Payne replied: "The time is at hand when the ministry of the A.M.E. Church must drive out this heathenish mode of worship or drive out all the intelligence, [the] refinement, and practical Christians who may be in her bosom."[4]

These and similar concerns probably led to the demise (or abandonment) of the ring shout in some places. However, descendants of Sea Island dwellers and other Africans along the coasts of South and North Carolina, Georgia, and Florida clearly affirm the "ring" and other forms of circular motion as a viable carryover from Africa. Therefore, forms of "ring rituals" have continued well into the twenty-first century. In an effort to keep such practices alive, ring dances and ring shouts are incorporated into wedding rituals of African Americans along with the ritual of "jumping the broomstick." Where communal circular formations are still practiced or newly introduced to communities of faith, the sense of *African continuity* is greatly emphasized! There are some who claim that the "holy dance," prevalent among African American Pentecostals, possibly originated in the ring shout. There is general consensus among musicians that the circular concept involving the community is a basic guideline for African instrumentalists. This form of communal interaction is dominant among jazz ensembles.[5]

For Discussion

1. The circle, in African traditions, symbolizes continuity, unity, and unbrokenness. Explore the effects of a ring shout with a small group as you sing one or more Spirituals such as "Glory, Glory, Hallelujah" (known also as "Since I Laid My Burden Down"), "In That Great Getting Up Morning," "Ain'ta Dat Good News?" or others that can be taught quickly. Clear a space wide enough to accommodate a large group circle. Encourage participants—shoulder to shoulder—and feel the bonding between you and other persons in the circle. Begin moving around in the circle, slowly at first, building momentum and speed as the group feels comfortable.

2. Have the group reflect on what they have just done and what they felt while doing it as well as what they feel now that the ring shout has ended.

3. The Black "meter" hymn tradition (or "Dr. Watts") developed into an art form that makes use of common meter, short meter, and long meter hymns with four lines of poetry. If this style of singing is unfamiliar to you, it would be well to listen to such singing before attempting to imitate it. The melodic line will not follow a prescribed musical pattern, but will vary according to the meaning of the text. The group might find that singing in this style will not only be interesting, but will also engender a deep religious feeling within the group.

CHAPTER 5

RITUALS, SACRAMENTS, AND ORDINANCES

Ritual action in the Christian community of faith is founded on actions and words of Jesus, which are imbued with hope and fulfillment. Slaves who embraced Christianity, deeply rooted in an awareness of the importance and necessity of community rituals, found new meaning in familiar social behavior. Continuity and identity with the ancient past and the present, prevalent in African rituals, were preserved in the light of God's action in Jesus the Christ. A hermeneutic of hope in a liberated future became the good news from God, who sides with the oppressed. Rituals of eating, drinking, and washing and rites of passage were imbued with the essence of the gospel message. The gathered African American church community, which already embraced the African ancestors (living dead) and the unborn, was extended to include those considered outside the immediate societal group as understood in the African world view.

Adapting and assimilating Christian concepts for slaves no doubt involved a slow ritualization process leading to a new understanding over a period of time: a period of separation from a previous living environment and resulting experiences of loneliness; a period of transition in a new world where life was viewed with suspicion; and incorporation into a new community that the participant helps shape and define. Later generations of Africans in America experienced the rites of passage with less confusion at liminal states when a definable African American community was available to facilitate rites of passage. Such rituals involved participation from the evangelizing community and engendered theological discussions about the meaning of the inclusivity of the body of Christ.

Baptism

Early North American history is replete with arguments pro and con among Protestant settlers regarding the baptism of slaves. Arguments against baptism were founded in the fear that baptism would force planters to emancipate their slaves and, therefore, weaken the planters' "cheap" work force. These arguments caused planters to vacillate between their Christian commission to preach the good news and baptize all nations and their strong inclination to protect their economic interests. Once this matter was solved by law, Protestant and Catholic colonists were able to consent to baptisms and still hold slaves in bondage. Some of the planters even stood as sponsors during slave baptisms. In Capuchin missions, Holy (Easter) Saturday and the Vigil of Pentecost were annual occasions for the baptizing of large groups of slaves and free African Americans. According to some records, as many as fifty to one hundred would be baptized in one day, often with only minimal catechizing.

Where efforts of evangelization and baptism were sincere, missionaries continued the struggle to catechize and free converted slaves. One plan was to begin the evangelization of Africa with converted slaves and free Blacks from America. Some of the serious evangelization efforts among some denominations were part of the Great Awakening. Quakers, who had the reputation of condemning slavery, set the pace for antislavery movements.

Through the centuries, certain "liturgical mannerisms" have obviously been important in attempts to cope with reality honestly and with integrity. The inherent religious African primal world views encourage actions toward the Holy Other that encompass an "advanced toward-shield from" dialectic. As indicated by Erwin Goodenough, worshipers "throw curtains between themselves and the tremendum, on which can be projected accounts of how the world came into existence, pictures of divine or superhuman forces or beings that control the universe, and us as well as codes of ethical behavior, and ritual which bring favor instead of catastrophe."[1]

Worshipers experience the ambiguity of wanting to encounter the mystery while wanting also to escape it. Since the Holy Spirit works according to divine rather than human will, there is always the possibility that the Spirit will break through and redirect the intentions of worshipers.

Regardless of the intentions and expectations of African Americans during worship, there are acts of preparation prior to Sunday morning that also reflect psychological attitudes. Saturday night "cleansing" rituals evidently started during slavery when some slaves were attending worship with slaveholders. Saturday night baths, laying out of Sunday clothes, and shining shoes are clearly evident from this period, and, in many instances, to the present. Worshipers evidently felt that it was necessary to appear before the Lord as physically clean and as dressed-up as possible. The preparation of Sunday dinner on Saturday, especially among rural worshipers, was also a ritual act that continued to be prevalent into the late 1950s. This freed those who cooked to be able to devote Sunday to worship activities, church singing festivals, and dinner on the church grounds, which often lasted well into Sunday evening. The puritanical idea that the Sabbath was to be dedicated to the Lord as a day of rest facilitated the shaping of unwritten African American laws about certain activities to avoid on Sunday, and it strengthened the concept of Sunday as a special day for spiritual formation and development. When there was to be no preaching at certain churches, it was appropriate for worshipers to meet for Sunday school and then attend church wherever there was preaching, regardless of the denomination. Walking was the most common mode of transportation, and many families would walk miles to participate in worship. Walking to church was functional as well as therapeutic.

Although there are no theological references in African American literature to every Sunday as Easter or Paschal celebrations, African Americans apparently lived as if they understood this concept. The everyday life of toil, so clouded with impending death imposed by the world, could be transcended on the Lord's Day when death had been overcome by the resurrection of Jesus.[2] Saturday "cleansing" preparations facilitated approaching God in order to attend to basic psychological needs expressed in worship: The need to experience

—mystery and meaning in God's transcendence and immanence;
—refuge and stability in a world of uprootedness;
—belongingness, compassion, and mutual fellowship with other members of the body of Christ;
—assurance of forgiveness and cleansing from sin and guilt as the soul is laid naked before God;
—peace, comfort, and release from tension, anxiety, and grief as finite beings in a confused world;
—healing from brokenness;
—fulfillment and wholeness; and
—joy in being found by God, who seeks.

African Heritage

Regardless of circumstances surrounding baptisms, the waters of Christian baptism for African adults and recently transported African children perhaps evoked memories of the symbolic use of water dominant in the African world view. Whether at a font, a baptismal pool, a large or small stream or creek, or a river, the converted slave could recall the unity of God's creation and the significance of water in the creation process. In many African societies, large bodies of water, rain, and waterfalls are evidence of God's continual creation and, therefore, sacred places where God meets humanity. Where water and rainfall are scarce, many African societies greet the rainy season with rituals of thanksgiving for God's perpetual expression of goodness. Rain, originating from above, links humanity with the divine.

Terms for "God" or "Supreme Being" in some African traditions are the same or quite similar to the term for "water" or "rain."[3] The use of water in African rites of passage with implications for Christian baptism has been documented elsewhere.[4] The symbolism is much like that of the Judeo-Christian tradition: cleansing, purification, death and dying, regeneration, new life, new birth, and re-creation. A consistent understanding is that in the "rhythm of life" one must pass through a form of death in order to move to another stage in the cycle of life. Each stage is marked by certain rites of passage that make the passage believable and unforgettable. The entire community—immediate and extended family—is invited to participate as nurturers and supporters of one moving into new responsibilities. In most, if not all, rites of passage, water or some liquid is used to communicate what is impossible to express with words.

Some slaves might have been familiar with river cults, river spirits, or water spirits in West Africa and could possibly have related these beliefs to Christian baptism. Melville J. Herskovits contends that baptism by immersion can be traced directly to water cults in Nigeria and Dahomey and, therefore, strongly appealed to African Americans who became Baptists or joined other denominations where immersion is the only mode of baptism. Much of his thesis breaks down, however, when other data and religious practices are examined.[5]

Catechesis

Since the theology and modes of baptism for each denomination vary, records are not always clear as to how much a slave convert or the slave family of an infant knew about what was taking place. Progress in preparing slaves for baptism was initially slow because of the objections of slaveholders to the evangelization of slaves and because of the process carried out by missionaries.

The Church of England, through the Society for the Propagation of the Gospel in Foreign Parts (S.P.G.), required religious instruction before baptism. The Society, founded in 1701, was a missionary arm of the Church of England that ministered to the American colonists and provided religious instructions for Native Americans and African American slaves. Their first efforts basically involved catechizing American-born slave children, but with little initial success. According to reports from some of the missionaries, slaves born in Africa were the most difficult to catechize, mainly because of language barriers. There was also the matter of resistance to religious instruction by some who could not understand the English language. Not all slaves were eager to accept Christianity.

The Reverend Samuel Thomas, a missionary of Goose Creek Parish in the colony of South Carolina, is noted as the first successful S.P.G. worker.[6] Thomas began his work in 1695, six years before the Society was established, and by 1705 he had instructed as many as one-thousand slaves. We are indebted to the Reverend Francis Le Jau for evidence of the catechetical method used. In 1710 Le Jau reported his work with slaves and Native Americans after regular service:

> We begin and end our particular assembly with the Collect "Prevent us
> O Lord," etc. I teach them the Creed, the Lord's Prayer, and the
> Commandments. I explain some portion of the catechism. I give them
> the liberty to ask questions. I endeavor to proportion my answers and all
> my instructions to their wants and capacity.[7]

Le Jau insisted upon two years of continuing catechesis before baptism and admittance to the Lord's Supper. Religious instruction included teaching the slaves to read, thus catechesis was equivalent to a general education. The declaration Le Jau prepared for adult slave candidates for baptism (cited on p. 21) provided evidence of limitations placed on slaves, because of the issues of baptism and freedom.

Schools for slaves gradually emerged, with preparation for baptism as a major focus. A school founded in New York under the leadership of lay catechist Elias Neau provided catechetical instructions, often from house to house. Many students were reported in 1720 to have made sufficient progress, so some were already baptized, and some were succeeding well in communicant classes. Whereas a few, reportedly, were not able to read, their memories were of such that they could recite the history of Creation, the Flood, the giving of the Law, and the birth, miracles, and Crucifixion of Jesus.[8]

In addition to the work of the Anglicans, other Protestant denominations as well as Catholics participated in providing religious instruction in the eighteenth and nineteenth centuries. The Reverend Charles C. Jones began his missionary work in 1831. One important aspect of his labors was the preparation of a *Catechism . . . for the Oral Instruction of Colored Persons*, published in 1834.[9] This document, like previous ones of its kind, however, urged obedience of slaves to masters.

As the Christian faith was reworked, authenticated, and internalized by African Americans, and as they were able to experience conversions and to participate in the religious instruction of their own people, catechesis became more meaningful. Raboteau observes that what was involved in the slaves' acceptance of Christianity was the slow process by which "Africans became New Negroes."[10] The major success of catechesis was a stimulation of critical and analytical thinking that allowed African Americans to find meaning in life, using the language and a vitally important book of the oppressors.

Practices

Slave baptisms apparently lifted the spirits of an oppressed people, engendering excitement in slave communities. In spite of restrictions on the mobility of slaves, attendance at baptisms seemed to have been generally acceptable. The news of a forthcoming baptism or "baptizing" traveled fast throughout the plantation and in neighboring slave communities. A part of the mystique surrounding this central act of worship was the sacred opportunity for fellowship for Christians and non-Christians. The enthusiasm was apparent whether participants observed baptisms by sprinkling or pouring at the font, from the vantage point of the balcony, or at the water's edge where they exploded into cathartic ecstasy as candidates were immersed.

Baptisms by immersion were particularly dramatic and celebrative. Both slave and free, representing many denominations, were known to have walked as far as ten miles to share in the excitement of these important and memorable occasions. One was not required to know the candidate(s); baptisms were events for all who were able and permitted to participate. This practice continued in the rural South well into the twentieth century as people in communities prepared themselves for the "baptizings" on certain Sundays of the year. These occasions—past and present—reveal many themes related to the African world view. There is an obvious assimilation of the African kinship system-fellowship, with an understanding of the theological themes of covenanted family, a sign and seal of incorporation in the mystical body of Christ and with one another. From an African perspective, the marking of anyone's passage from one stage to another is a cause for communal celebration. People generally like to witness the change that takes place in rituals of death and regeneration. The presence of others who show concern is in itself nurturing. There is also the joy of "just having a good time in the Lord," about which many participants can attest.

Some believers experienced a "transforming moment" and were considered "saved" prior to baptism. Other believers, in preparation for baptism, confessed their sins and indicated a desire to be saved. It was not unusual for slaves to beg forgiveness of persons whom they had offended, and forgive those who had offended them. Isaiah Jeffries, an ex-slave from South Carolina, relates this phase of his mother's preparation for baptism: "She went arond all de people dat she had done wrong and begged dere forgiveness. She sent fer dem dat had wronged her, and told dem she was born again and a new woman, and dat she would forgive dem. She wanted everybody dat was not saved to go up wid her."[11]

If, during the baptismal service, the candidate appeared to be in an "in-between-state," the community would sing, pray, and shout to "help them pass through." With the divine passage before, after, or during baptism, the onlookers would express their joy in shouts of jubilation. Talk about the baptizing experience would continue in the community for a long period of time.

Mass baptisms of large numbers of slaves are known to have occurred following revivals and camp meetings. Ex-slaves seemed to have delighted in describing some of these occasions: "Dey dammed up the crick on Sadday so as it would be deep enough on Sunday, and de done de baptizin' 'fore de three o'clock sermon. At dem baptizin's dere was all sorts of shoutin', and dey would sing *Roll Jordan, Roll, De Livin' Waters,* and *Lord I'se Comin' Home.*"[12]

Candidates, dressed in white and escorted to the pond or local "crick" by others who had been baptized, could hardly contain themselves before the pastor "ducked" them in the waters of death and resurrection.

Transformed and renewed, the newly baptized sometimes emerged from the water shouting "Hallelujah, thank you, Jesus!" or similar affirmations in recognition of their transforming moment. In many of the instances cited by slaves, preaching followed the baptism ceremony.

Notwithstanding the fact that there were more Baptists among the slave population, there are records of a large number of baptisms in other denominations. John Bachman, a Lutheran pastor, baptized more than two thousand African Americans during his years as pastor in Charleston, South Carolina. Some came as adults; others came as infants in the arms of their slave parents.[13] Both slave and free African Americans often served as godparents of infants at Episcopal and Roman Catholic churches. Euro-Americans would sometimes stand with African American parents as sponsors or godparents for slave children.[14]

Spirituals of this era that express the slaves' understanding of baptism include:

—"Cert'ny Lord" or "Certainly Lord," which includes the question, "Have you been baptized?"
—"Honor, Honor," which begins "King Jesus lit the candle by the waterside, to see the little children when they're truly baptized. . . . Oh, run along children, be baptized, might pretty meeting by the waterside. . . ."
—"Pray On!" which includes the lines, "In the river of Jordan, John baptized, How I long to be baptized. . . ."
—"Take Me to the Water (to Be Baptized)"
—"Wade in the Water"
—"Live a-Humble"

The Lord's Supper

There is less documentation of slave involvement in the celebration of the Lord's Supper. One significant account is provided by Erskine Clarke, whose research includes numerous primary resources. His description of "A Slave's Sabbath" in 1845 affirms the importance of both baptism and communion.[15] African Americans who had been baptized and received into the fellowship of any Protestant church could participate in the Lord's Supper. Many would have been familiar with the catechism of Charles C. Jones and would have heard and accepted the fact that for

(Protestant) Christians the Lord's Supper is an outward sign of their union with Christ, showing to all the world the death of Christ for sin. They might not have believed that it was also a visible sign of "mutual love and fellowship as members of the same mystical body," for there was too much evidence that those who taught this concept neither believed it nor practiced it.[16]

The example cited below by Clarke is from the Presbyterian tradition in Charleston, South Carolina, a practice that began as early as 1814.[17] Communion tokens were required of Lord's Supper participants, a practice of the Church of Scotland. A service of preparation was held during the week prior to the celebration, at which time those desiring Communion would be questioned as to their piety and Christian discipline.[18] One can assume that there would be separate preparatory services for slaves. Slave or free, Communion tokens for African Americans differed from those of Euro-Americans: Silver tokens were given to Euro-Americans, and pewter to African Americans. Slaves holding the silver token are known to have been punished.

Celebration of the Lord's Supper, whenever it occurred in interracial worship services, followed the preaching of the Word, with Euro-American members coming first to be served at the Table. African Americans with tokens would be served last. Coming down from the balcony or from their reserved section in the church, they would sit around the Lord's Table, present their tokens, and receive the bread and wine. Having been served, "they remained seated . . . in the midst of the white slave holders and in the center of the church until the conclusion of the final meditation."[19]

Apparently the Lord's Supper was not celebrated in the earliest Invisible Institutions and Praise Houses. One can speculate that celebrations might have occurred in interracial worship settings where ordained preachers served as celebrants. Although the information is rather scant, there is evidence that the First African Baptist Church of Savannah by 1850 "commemorated the Lord's Supper once every three months." Details are not provided, but the ritual action might have been similar to that of the majority of Baptist churches.[20]

In spite of historical exclusions from the Lord's Table prepared by early evangelizers, African Americans affirm the centrality of the Lord's Supper as a locus of liturgical discipline. The numerous instances of Jesus' eating, drinking, and interacting with common folks must have strengthened the importance of the holy meal for African Americans. One concerned for the hunger of five thousand would surely include ordinary people around a common table. One who deliberately seeks to invite the poor to dinner and welcomes tax collectors and sinners to eat with him would surely share a meal with social outcasts of any age and culture. It is no wonder then that the ritual of eating and drinking with Jesus, though varied in practice, focuses on God's self-giving and liberating act in and through Jesus the Christ.

Marriage

In spite of the nebulous state of "married" slaves in the colonies, there are records of wedding ceremonies of some kind on plantations. For slaves, marriages did not prevent or transcend the threat of separation by sales inherent in the slave system. Marriages were not recognized by law and were, therefore, dependent on the will and attitude of the slaveholder. For the slaveholder, marriage of slaves presented an irreconcilable conflict: the legitimacy of slavery and the necessity of legalizing relationships through marriage.[21]

A Christian marriage was intended to publicly announce and solemnize the love and union, under God, of two persons who were committed to live together until death. The uncertainty of slave marriages contradicted this notion. Some slave weddings were ritualized according to the Christian understanding of unity under God. Some involved the use of an assimilation of forms of African and Christian rituals. Others, most often held without the approval of slaveholders, involved an assimilation of African and African American ritual patterns.

Practices

Weddings were held wherever it seemed most appropriate, whether in a place named by the bride and groom, the home of the preacher, the church, or the home of the slaveholder. There were "house" slaves who were privileged to have weddings supported and financed by slaveholders. One such wedding was described in 1862 by a Louisiana slaveholder who helped in the wedding preparations:

> Two of the servants got married (here tonight). The bride looked quite nice dressed in white. I made her turban of white swiss pink tartan and

orange blossoms. There were married at the gallery. . . . They afterwards adjourned to the "hospital" where they enjoyed a "ball." . . . The groom had on a suite of black, [with] white gloves and tall beaver. The bride was dressed in white swiss, pink trimmings and white gloves. The bridesmaid and groom's man were dressed to correspond.[22]

The ritual of "jumping the broomstick" is also cited as a part of the wedding ceremony, most often separate from the Christian solemnization of a marriage. The broomstick ritual was occasionally added to the regular ceremony at the request of slaves who felt that this act authenticated the regular rite. Some couples, with the slaveholder's permission, merely "jumped the broomstick" and were declared married. This ritual involved the bride and groom facing each other, each placing a broom on the floor in front of them. At the appropriate time they would step across their broom simultaneously and take hold of the other's hand. This was an act of declaration of marriage and was as binding as a marriage performed by a minister. A variation of this method required one broom that was held ten to twelve inches off the floor by one person at each end. The bride and groom, one after the other, would jump backward over the broom as a declaration of marriage.

Some slaveholders assumed the authority to tell slave couples that they were married. The verbal "pronouncement" was the official "rite of passage," thus a public wedding ritual was considered unnecessary. After emancipation, some slaves had their marriages "legalized" by purchasing a license and holding a service under the authority of a pastor. Regardless of circumstances or form of ritual, some slaves looked upon their marriage to a single person as permanent and binding. In other instances, multiple marriages were viewed as acceptable, since there was no law that held them to one person.

Funerals

Slaves, like their African ancestors, took death seriously, and therefore placed great emphasis on the funerary rites of passage. For a people whose past and present had been disrupted by slave ships and threatened by premature deaths and auction blocks, death provided a form of relief from a world of sorrow. It was also assurance of hope for a brighter tomorrow for those who would in death, like their ancestors, live closer to God. Death meant for some slaves a return home to Africa and a state of happier existence. Rather than a passage from life to an unknown state, death might have represented transition from bondage to freedom, from hell to heaven. Africans in a new world were intentional in the celebration of life as they dignified death.

During the early years, African rituals were very much in evidence at funerals and burials, especially in the rural, southeastern part of the United States. The wholeness of the sacred cosmos, with the living and the "living dead" connected by spirits, seems to have been the operating African world view. In a strange and alien land, beliefs in "spirits" and the spirit world continued strongly in connection with death, where fear and awe operate simultaneously. Over the years, with the shaping of a unique African American Christianity, many of these practices were discontinued or assimilated into Judeo-Christian ideas and rituals. One example of this fusion, reportedly from Mississippi, is a practice that connected Hallowe'en, the eve of All Saints Day in the Western Christian tradition, and African beliefs in spirits.[23] In order to quell the roaming activities of "hungry" spirits on Hallowe'en, food was cooked and placed on the table with the necessary serving utensils. During the night the "essence" or "spirit" of the food would be devoured by hungry spirits. The placing of cooked food on graves for the spirits is reported in numerous Southern communities.

Practices

Early in slave history, gatherings for funerals were both greatly feared and held in awe by slaveholders. The celebrative dignity of the ceremonies of a people enslaved must have been awesome, especially for onlookers; however, there was also fear induced by conspiracies that were known to have been plotted at funerals. For this reason, in 1687 public funerals were banned in parts of Virginia. In 1772, the corporation of the City of New York required that funerals be held during daylight hours, with no more than twelve persons present.[24] These fears were not unwarranted. The plot for the Gabriel Prosser insurrection of 1800 was organized during the funeral of a child. In spite of this, funerals were very often permitted. Some were limited to a simple rite such as marching around the grave three times and the "mumbling" of words, possibly of African origin, that the African American community appeared to understand.

Permission was required to hold funeral services that were often held at night, especially in the South where there were heavy concentrations of African Americans. The more practical reason for this was to avoid interference with the slave's daily work requirements. There was also a prevailing belief that the spirit of the deceased remained with the body until daybreak, then it went home to God as the stars disappeared.[25] The family—extended family and friends—kept vigil (held a wake) all night, mourning the deceased in song, prayer, and silence; but they were expected to assume their daily chores at daybreak.

Where funerals were held during the day, slaves were quite willing to give up their regular activities on Sunday to attend. Funeral services were sometimes held separately from burials, with burials preceding funerals. The length of time between the two services would vary from several days to weeks or months, depending on the mitigating circumstances surrounding the death, or whatever was expedient for the slaveholder. The reason for two separate services might also have been rooted in the African world view that assumed that proper attention must be given to the deceased. A hasty funeral rite of passage at death would not assure appropriate entrance of the dead into the spirit world. Thus a delayed funeral would be more efficacious than a hurried one.

When a person died, the slave community generally followed a procedure much like that found in sections of Africa. If time permitted, the body was laid out on a cooling board to be prepared for the funeral and burial. The body of a female was wrapped in a winding sheet, whereas male bodies were wrapped in a black shroud as in some West African traditions.[26] Bodies were attended by family and members of the community until the funeral and burial plans were made. In an effort to make the soul "rest easy," so that it would not return to haunt the family and friends, mourners talked to the deceased on the assumption that the soul could hear what was said. As they said their farewells, the body was often touched by members of the family and mourners.

A "proper" funeral rite was necessary to further put the spirit of the deceased to rest, and to ensure against the return of the spirit to "disturb" the living. In some West African cultures, a second burial or memorial was held so that the entire community could participate, further assuring the proper rest for the spirit of the "living dead." The delay in holding funerals might have reflected a continuation of this tradition. It might also have been the uncertainty or fear inherent in the slave system, which would not assure the uninterrupted length of time necessary for the rite of passage. Another more practical reason might have been the rapidity of decay of the human body, which necessitated a hasty burial. In an effort to protect their dead, slaves could not subject the unembalmed body to heat, which caused decay and subsequent encroachment of vultures.

From the account of witnesses, slave funerals were highly ceremonial. Generally, a long procession of mourners walked slowly from the house of the deceased to the place of the service, with lighted torches made from pine knots or made from rags saturated with kerosene tied around tree branches or discarded handles of workers' tools. The procession was led by a pastor, pall bearers, and sometimes the slave master. The practice of the community's walking with the dead to the final resting place has in the African counterpart the symbolization of the shared journey of the living and the dead. Each person walking was comforted knowing that he or she, too, would be equally respected. The wooden coffins usually remained open throughout the service as the slave community bade farewell to one of its members. Songs, prayers, and words about the deceased were expressed in mournful wailing tones and "wild chants," with a deep sense of grief and respect, mixed with consolation.

Preaching

Slave masters are known to have preached at some of these services, but slave preachers were preferred. The depth of the emotional need and an immeasurable amount of time required to "authenticate" the rite was conceivably best understood by an African American. Black preachers often gained reputations as great orators because of their excellent leadership at funerals. The description of the expertise of John Jasper, a renowned preacher in Virginia, also documents evidence of the emotional impact of slave funerals:

> A negro funeral without an uproar, without shouts and groans, without fainting women and shouting men, without pictures of triumphant deathbeds and judgement day and without the gates of heaven wide open and the subjects of the funeral dressed white and rejoicing around the throne of the Lamb, was no funeral at all. Jasper was a master from the outset at this work. One of his favorite texts, as a young preacher, was that which was recorded in Revelations, sixth chapter, and second verse. . . . Before the torrent of his florid and spectacular eloquence the people were swept down to the ground, and sometimes for hours many seemed to be in trances, not a few lying as if they were dead.[27]

Preachers like Jasper facilitated the "necessary" catharsis that allowed mourners to travel with the deceased to the gates of heaven where they could glimpse the happy state of others who had died. These brief journeys created visions of hope in the eschatological future where all would be well. Following the sermon and ecstasy, believers would claim to have visited with deceased kin in heaven and would be assured that their own death would be acceptable or bearable. The body might be buried in death, but the spirit returns to the original spiritual place where life is eternal, and in which the living can participate. In such an emotional state, the living receive legitimation as they are assured of their own somebodiness. At such high moments they were granted a new meaning of life and ultimate death and were renewed to continue life, albeit a form of hell on earth.

Some funerals of slaves and ex-slaves were deliberately orchestrated to allow this form of catharsis to take place. It was not unusual for mourners to shout, engage in ritual dancing to the rhythm of the fiery preaching, clap their hands, sing enthusiastically, and, where allowed, play percussive instruments.

Burials

Burial rites were important in traditional West African societies where the veneration of ancestors was prevalent. Not only was the funeral ceremony an integral part of community life, but also proper care was given to the interment of the deceased. Vestiges of this tradition continued into the New World and were assimilated into Christian beliefs and practices. The graves of early African Americans were often dug in an east-west direction. The coffin was placed so that the head was west and the feet east, with the explanation that when Gabriel blows his trumpet in the eastern sunrise, the dead could rise up and walk toward the east without having to turn around. Another explanation given by ex-slaves is that a person should not sleep or be buried "cross-ways of the world." This tradition appears to be more African than European, although the importance of the east in ecclesiastical directions has been maintained throughout the history of Christianity. In both instances, the practice is related to the direction of the rising of the sun as the source of light, life, and goodness.

Practices

The African practice of "decorating" graves with broken pottery, pieces of glass, and some personal belongings of the deceased was continued by slaves in the rural South, notably on the Sea Islands of South Carolina, Georgia, and in Mississippi. The broken pieces symbolized for the African both the freeing of the spirit of the dead to leave the earth and the ease with which the broken pieces could be carried by the spirit. Broken pieces also symbolized the destruction of the body by death. Personal belongings of the deceased were placed there to "lay the spirit," so there would be no need for the spirit to return to the house for them.

There was also a custom in the southeast of throwing dirt into the grave at funerals, which might also have African roots. The symbolism and significance of this custom are not clear; however, it has been identified as a "negro" custom that was used by some Euro-American Southerners.

Current burial practices in Africa engender natural speculation that the custom could be connected to rituals in East Africa, where the entire community remains as the coffin is buried under the dirt and is cemented over. Conversation at the grave site is generally about the virtues of the deceased. The family is first to sprinkle or carefully place flowers on the freshly cemented grave, followed by the placing of flowers by the community. Burial rites among the Nyoro of Uganda include the sprinkling of the first dirt in the grave by the children of the deceased. Dirt is to be scooped up with their hands, after first brushing a little with their elbows, three times for the mother, four for the father. The significance of this custom is that the survivors' hands are no longer of use to the deceased, since they can no longer carry out their proper function of serving those who are now deceased. The custom of throwing dirt in the grave may be connected with the custom of sprinkling dirt on the coffin, currently in use in some places, symbolizing the dust and clay from which the human body was made and to which it ultimately returns.

A practice that persists even today at some burials on the Sea Islands and in Charleston, South Carolina, is the passing of young children over the coffin of a deceased parent at the grave site. If the body has been returned to the home of the deceased, the passing of young children over the coffin could take place before the body is returned to the hearse en route to the funeral. The reason given for this ritual act is to free the spirit of the deceased to leave the earth in peace. If the spirit of the deceased parent is not freed, it will haunt the young children and literally "worry" them to an early death. Although this exact ritual cannot be traced to specific societies in West Africa, similar practices have been observed among the Bush Negroes of Dutch Guiana. Children of the deceased play important roles in a number of West African societies, as indicated above.

Another custom in South Carolina, continuing from the slave period, is to allow children to march around the casket of the deceased father, singing a hymn, after which the youngest is passed over and then under the casket. The casket is then taken out and "run upon" the shoulders of two men.[28] The young men run with the corpse through the village. A similar practice has been traced to the Dahomey of West Africa.[29]

Music

Enthusiastic singing during the funeral was replaced with slow, somber singing en route to the cemetery. After the burial, a more festive air was assumed, and the music was usually faster and lighter. By the time mourners reached the home of the deceased or other designated place, the festive mood would have heightened for a celebrative meal, which often included fermented beverages. Celebrations may have continued until dawn.

When the use of instruments was allowed, instrumentalists joined the procession and played slow, mournful hymns or Spirituals. In Southern cities where brass bands were available, they were often invited to provide music. The improvisatory skills of jazz bands were developed in the process, especially in and around New Orleans.

Processionals to and recessions from the graveyard are reminiscent of funeral practices in Africa. It is likely that these memories were from those recently transported from Africa.

Burials and funerals were considered especially "grand" and dignified when both respect for the deceased and status for the living were demonstrated. In addition to marking the final rite of passage for the dead, funerals and burials were social events and a kind of sacralized therapy necessary for family, friends, and the community to "live on."

Funeral Societies and Burial Associations

Free African Americans set the pace for elaborate and expensive funerals prior to emancipation. Elaborate practices requiring expensive burial policies have continued into the twenty-first century with the assimilation of contemporary ideas and developments in mortuary customs. These practices reflect an awareness, on the part of the morticians and families, of the fusion of African and Judeo-Christian traditions.

Funeral societies, burial associations, or "bands" were organized in the North and South by free African Americans to ensure "decent" funerals and burials. Euro-Americans were always suspicious of these societies out of fear that any secret African American groups would provide an arena for organizing plans for insurrections. The earliest evidence of an organization that had as one of its concerns "mutual aid" to assist those in need was the Free African Society. It was founded in Philadelphia in 1787 by African American pioneers in the building of "visible" institutions predicated on the concerns of African Americans. Two societies, The Sons of the African Society, organized in Boston in 1789, and the Brown Fellowship Society, established in Charleston, South Carolina, in 1790, were established mainly to assure decent funerals and burials for their members. The Brown Fellowship Society was more specific in its purpose to establish a fund to relieve its members in hours of distress, sickness, and death. Careful minutes of each meeting were kept and published with its membership list in 1844.[30]

Members of this society were among the wealthiest of free people of color in Charleston. The purchase of a cemetery lot and the building of a society hall provided visible evidence of the work of this organization. This society was also known to be among the most conservative in political outlook; therefore, it was not so suspect as other burial associations in the South. Nevertheless, some of the white churches, in an effort to counteract potential insurrections, provided their African American members opportunities to hold funeral services and also arranged for separate burial grounds. Of the fifteen "colored cemeteries" in Charleston in 1856, one belonged to the two African American burial societies (Brown Fellowship Society and Humane Brotherhood, the darker skinned, more liberal free people of color), two were owned by the city, and the others were owned by Euro-American churches.[31] With reference to burying grounds, the Burying Ground Society of Free People of Color of Richmond, Virginia, established in 1815, was known for its commitment to assist families in planning ahead for funerals and burials.[32]

With concerted efforts, African Americans were assured of a proper and decent burial place. "Going home" would remain a time of jubilee for the entire African American community, as African Americans served as preachers, mortuary officiants, and participants. The deceased had surely crossed over the "river" into the "promised land," as those who remained in slavery had to return to the struggles of daily toil.

For Discussion

1. Share some of the meaningful family rituals that have helped sustain the unity of your family.

2. Identify some of the symbols and ritual actions incorporated in the rites of baptism or the Lord's Supper that are unique to your culture.

3. Jesus used familiar symbols from his culture—water, bread, and cup—as basic reminders of his life and ministry. What symbols would you add from particular cultures that broaden your understanding of the Christian faith?

4. The act of "jumping the broom" or jumping over an imaginary line also symbolizes the leap into new life as husband and wife. What additional practices related to this ritual affirm the importance of the family and community in support of this "leap"?

CHAPTER 6

ORIGINS AND PRACTICES OF AFRICAN AMERICAN DENOMINATIONS AND CONGREGATIONS

W e really 'had church' today!" is a familiar expression among African Americans following a Spirit-filled worship experience. The implication of this folksy phrase is that the Spirit of God had moved with such power that all social barriers were removed and worshipers were able to "have a good time in the Lord." The passionate, celebrative style of preaching had no doubt reached the depth of worshipers' souls and had "set them on fire!" The Word of God in sermon and song had spoken to the conditions of the gathered community, who could say emphatically that they had "heard a word from the Lord." Prayers were no doubt spontaneously offered by worshipers who were gifted in the oratorical skill of "turning and tuning" familiar phrases so that God's liberating acts in history could find meaning for the moment. Often, the anticipated good news would cause the church to "rock" as many worshipers responded with their whole beings. Although the "church" having a good time might be identified with a particular denomination, the worshipers represent a variety of denominations.

The genius of Black worship is its openness to the creative power of God that frees and enables people, regardless of denomination, to "turn themselves loose" and celebrate God's act in Jesus Christ. In the process, worshipers are inspired to be creative. Indeed, traditional African American worship can be viewed as a spiritual art form. The drama inherent in worship lends itself naturally to joyful glorification and enjoyment of God. This is *not* to say that *all* Black worship is designed to be entertaining, nor are all worship experiences filled with physical excitement. Stereotyping of worship undermines mission and ministry, so important in the Black community. There *is* a balance in African American worship forms that is most often identified by denominational distinctions and geographical differences.

Much more has been written and confirmed about traditional African American denominations than about African American congregations in Euro-American denominations.[1] It is true that African American denominations have been a major stabilizing force in the Black community. Nevertheless, the term "Black church" also includes African American congregations functioning separately from their Euro-American parent churches. To overlook any African American contributors to social change and liturgical life severs the inherent unity of African Americans wherever they find themselves.

The fact that separate congregations were necessary is no less important than the need for separate African American denominations. In both instances, the need for separate places of worship was created because of societal injustices and inequities. By the fact of their existence, both separate African American denominations and African American congregations in Euro-American denominations attest to the concern and need for sincere love and unity in the beloved family of God. African Americans who choose Euro-American denominations are just as "marginalized" by society as are members of Black denominations.

Worship, when and wherever it occurs, provides opportunities for the hope of members to be raised in the face of adversity. The racial ethnic context allows diversity to be viewed as an asset rather than a hindrance to a natural, uninhibited response to God's grace. A sense of wholeness is facilitated when worshipers can bring all that they are to the beloved community and know that they will be appreciated and affirmed. The manner of ritual action (the *how*) must take into consideration the context (the *where*) as the gathered community generates and redefines order through the experience of the divine. Richard Wright states this more poetically: "Our churches are where we dip our tired bodies in cool springs of hope, where we retain our wholeness and humanity despite the blows of death."[2]

Functioning at first as a clandestine body, African Americans in worship were not bound by predetermined theologies of worship or predetermined models of Christian ritual action. For this historical gathering, worship happened as a process by which the gathered community alternated or moved freely between fixed and evolving worlds of behavior. Without an awareness or concern for the concept of *oikumene*, the initial nondenominational group became unified as it determined its own limits or boundaries for ritual action, based on prior African rituals and existential needs. Such self-imposed boundaries allowed worshipers to transcend imposed societal structures as they generated new models of ritual behavior or "anti-structures."[3] In this way, worship provided an optional form of life "on the margin," in sacred space where familiar cultural symbols could be utilized in the shaping of rituals.

The corporate worship of God through ritual action involves people in relationship with one another. Unhealthy societal structures can be transcended in worship as the gathered community, consciously or subconsciously, reacts to established structures while generating new ones. Modes of expression that are unique to African American worshipers are imbued with the power to replace some of the enforced political models at the controlling center of society. Spiritually "high" moments generated by the ecstasy and intensity in worship are liminal or marginal experiences where the social status of the community has been redefined. The unique modes of responding—praying, preaching, singing, gathering, and greeting—foster and nurture the anti-structural dimension of social awareness.

Continuing in the tradition of those who established African American worship traditions, contemporary worshipers relate dialectically and paradoxically to the world in their responses to God. A "good time in the Lord" induces a change-invoking power that elevates worshipers above the contradictions of an oppressive society. Anti-structures created by and for the powerless are arenas where hope and faith, inherent in the Word of God, can find natural responses. The common African heritage and the socialization process in a racist society provide the foundation for many aspects of worship that connect African Americans and transcend denominational labels.

The desire and hunger for freedom and wholeness, which permeated the marginalized slave community, continues into the twenty-first century. Worship, separate from an oppressing society, provides opportunities for ecstatic modes of ritual that help free one's thoughts and revitalize the hope inherent in the gospel. The experience of sacred awe and adoration of the holy apart from, yet in the midst of, a hypocritical environment, transforms both individual and group worshipers. It is no wonder, then, that celebration of the presence and power of God in uniquely structured and spontaneous prayers, sermons, and songs is filled with expressions of thanksgiving "for yet another time to have church!" or "be in the house of the Lord."

African Americans who commonly experienced the merging of societal problems and moral conflicts found temporary relief in ritual action. One could cathartically experience tension and release, fear and freedom, sadness and joy, and emerge with a sense of wholeness. Celebrations of the acts of God in history are realized in God's divine acts of liberation at the present moment. Verbal and nonverbal communication between God and humanity facilitates human-to-human communication. The community is enabled by the power of the Holy Spirit to enter and reenter God's story, and experience the oneness of the body of Christ without fear of degradation.

These common worship trends persist in corporate African American worship in varying degrees, both in African American denominations as well as in congregations in historically Euro-American denominations. Without question, the emergence of African American denominations provides major visible evidence of institutional liberation movements initiated by an oppressed people. Sufficient evidence has been cited to attest to the historical need for African Americans to be liberated from Euro-American church control in a pseudo-interracial, slave-worshiping environment. The matter of ecclesiastical and liturgical equality for African American worshipers was hardly considered by eighteenth- and nineteenth-century slaveholders! Opportunities for slaves to worship with slaveholders often expanded the means for controlling servants, while limiting their religious freedom. What better place than specially built lofts, "high and lifted-up," could slaves be situated for constant monitoring? What opportunity was more appropriate than a "segregated time for prayer" in worship for Richard Allen and Absalom Jones to walk out in a visible declaration of liturgical independence?

The Role of Pioneer African American Preachers

The unique contributions of particular worship leaders are beyond the scope of this book. However, the important role of a few African American preachers must be reviewed briefly, because they were pioneers in many liturgical endeavors. Their commitment and ability to proclaim a message of hope, not only to an oppressed people but to those who were among the oppressors, attests to their response to God's call to be open channels of divine communication. They were also leaders in the shaping and perpetuation of the Invisible Institution, the founding of denominations, and in the establishing of African American congregations in Euro-American denominations.

Prior to and following the emergence of African American denominations and congregations in Euro-American denominations, African American preachers were recognized for their unusual oratory and homiletical skills. Some preachers were granted permission to preach in Euro-American congregations. An "official" preacher needed a license from a church, which was given for a specific area or for a more extended outreach for a limited period of time. Many respected and powerful preachers were neither ordained nor licensed, but were allowed to serve as "exhorters."[4]

It is believed that African American women were among the powerful preachers in clandestine settings, although there is very little recorded evidence of their activities. Prior to the late nineteenth century, none of the pioneer women preachers were ever officially acknowledged. A posthumous publication of a tract by Philadelphia Quakers in 1889 relates the story of a woman preacher in Maryland, known only as Elizabeth (1766?–84), who began to preach at the age of thirty (ca. 1796).[5] Having neither an official license nor ordination, Elizabeth preached in spite of the constant threat of being arrested. Another pioneering woman preacher, Jarena Lee (b. 1783), was not ordained by her denomination, but served as an exhorter.[6] Because of opposition received from her denomination, Rebecca Cox Jackson (1795–1871) joined the Quakers, where her prophetic and preaching gifts were accepted.[7] Amanda Berry Smith (1837–1915) was also among the earliest Black women preachers whose leadership helped shape African American worship traditions.[8]

Whether lay, licensed, or ordained, Black preachers (male and female) were vanguards in shaping and perpetuating folk traditions that undergird African American worship. As spiritual leader, politician, priest, prophet, and storyteller, the preacher knew how to take advantage of opportunities to teach what was needed about social situations and personhood.

Black (male) preachers were highly visible in the community and were generally elevated to a position of authority and power by the Black community. During slavery, the preacher, called of God, was granted a few social privileges denied other slaves. Although deterred somewhat by the lack of an "authorized" education, the slave preacher learned basic biblical rudiments and utilized the skills of eloquence in interpreting the Word to the people. Endowed with the gifts of an unusual memory, a vivid imagination, and a capacity for poetic turning of phrases, Black preachers could hold the attention of a congregation while engendering fervent emotional excitement. The natural spiritual depth of their art was apparently contagious. As one observer noted in 1862:

> The real spiritual benefit of these poor people, instrumentally, seems to have been mostly derived from a sort of local preachers, Colored, and mostly slaves, but of deep spiritual experience, sound sense and capacity to state Scripture facts, narratives, and doctrines, far better than most, who feed upon commentaries. . . . True, most of them could not read, still, some of them line hymns from memory with great accuracy and fervor. . . . Their teaching shows clearly that it is God in the soul, that makes the religious teacher. One is amazed with their correctness and power.[9]

Numerous narratives of ex-slave preachers indicate that this unusual gift was of divine origin rather than having been humanly acquired. The slave community accepted the Word of the Lord from the preacher because the slaves perceived that the message, the messenger, and the mode of delivery were Spirit-directed and Spirit-filled. Whenever African Americans of unusual power preached with such force that Euro-Americans were also moved, steps were often taken to "silence" them. It is understandable, then, that leadership for the establishing of separate worshiping congregations and ultimately separate denominations stemmed primarily from the efforts of pioneering preachers. Such power from the pulpit was apparent in each denomination where preaching by African Americans was permitted.

The Origin of Separate Congregations and Denominations

Some African American congregations in Euro-American denominations were established before the Independent Black Church movement.

The first Black congregation on record was the "Bluestone" African Baptist church, organized in 1758 on the plantation of William Byrd on the Bluestone River near what is now Mecklenburg, Virginia.[10] Under the leadership of George Leile, a slave, a second Black church was organized in Silver Bluff, South Carolina, in the mid to latter half of the eighteenth century. The official organizing date is uncertain. Historian Carter G. Woodson reported the founding "between the years 1773 and 1775."[11] However, a cornerstone on the church indicates a founding date of 1750.[12]

The following chart of founding dates of congregations and denominations provides a historical chronology of the evolution of separate African American worshiping bodies from the mid-eighteenth to the mid-twentieth centuries.[13]

Historical Evolution of African American Congregations and Denominations

(Asterisks indicate founding dates of denominations.)

Date	Congregation/Denomination	Location
1758	African Baptist Church (Bluestone)	Luneburg (Mecklenburg), VA
1773/75?	African Baptist Church	Silver Bluff, SC
1784	Oldest Black Catholic parish	St. Augustine, FL, Territory
1794	African American Episcopal congregation	Philadelphia, PA
1794	African Zoar Methodist congregation First African American congregation in the Methodist Episcopal Church	Philadelphia, PA
1794	Bethel A.M.E. Church Joined with other churches to become the A.M.E. denomination in 1816	Philadelphia, PA

Date	Congregation/Denomination	Location
1796	A.M.E. Zion Chapel	New York, NY
1805	Ezion Methodist Episcopal Church	Wilmington, DE
*1805	Union American Methodist Episcopal Church, Inc. Traces its origin to the Ezion Methodist Church, which severed its ties with the Methodist Episcopal Church in 1813	Wilmington, DE
1807	First African American congregation of the Presbyterian Church	Philadelphia, PA
1813	Union Church of African Members	Wilmington, DE
*1816	African Methodist Episcopal Church	Philadelphia, PA
*1820	African Methodist Episcopal Zion Church	New York, NY
1829	First African American congregation among Congregationalists	New Haven, CT
1834	First African American congregation in the Christian Church (Disciples of Christ)	Midway, KY
*1863	Seventh-Day Adventist African American Seventh-Day Adventists claim membership from the founding date.	Battle Creek, MI
*1865	Colored Primitive Baptists of America	Columbia, TN

Date	Congregation/Denomination	Location
*1867	United American Free Will Baptist Denomination, Inc.	Green County, NC
1869	Colored Cumberland Presbyterian Church	Huntsville, AL
*1870	Christian Methodist Episcopal Church (formerly Colored Methodist Episcopal Church)	Jackson, TN
1871	Church of Christ (Disciples of Christ) An African American body that is autonomous from the majority Euro-American Christian Church (Disciples of Christ)	Lenoir County, NC
*1874	Second Cumberland Presbyterian Church (current name: Cumberland Presbyterian Church in America)	Huntsville, AL
1876	First African American congregation of the Dutch Reformed Church	Orangeburg, SC
*1885	National Baptist Convention of America, Inc.	Shreveport, LA
*1889	Church of the Living God (Christian workers for Fellowship) Believes that Jesus was Black, based on the lineage of Abraham and David	Oklahoma City, OK
*1894	Church of God in Christ, Inc. (Pentecostal) Founded in 1894 and incorporated in 1907	Memphis, TN

Date	Congregation/Denomination	Location
*1894/98	Church of Christ (Holiness), USA	Jackson, MS
*1895	National Baptist Convention USA, Inc.	Nashville, TN
*1897	Church of God in Christ (Holiness)	Lexington, MS
*1897/1901	Church of God (Apostolic), Inc.	Danville, KY
*1901	Church of God (Sanctified)	Columbia, TN
*1903	House of God, which is the Church of the Living God, The Pillar and Ground of the Truth, Without Controversy, Inc.	Dickson, TN
*1905	Free Christian Zion of Christ Church	Redemption, AR
1907	Church of God in Christ (Pentecostal) First incorporated body of Pentecostals	Memphis, TN
*1908	Fire Baptized Holiness Church of the Americas	Anderson, SC
*1961	Progressive National Baptist Convention, Inc.	Akron, OH
1969	Reformed Church in America Related to the Dutch Reformed Church	New York, NY
*1988	National Missionary Baptist Convention of America	Los Angeles, CA
*1989	African American Catholic Congregation Declared independence from the Roman Catholic Church in 1990	Washington, DC

As indicated above, the independent denominational movement was initially confined to Baptist and Methodist traditions. Although there are numerous speculations among Black church historians, the general consensus is that the simplicity of presentation of the gospel message, simplicity of worship styles, as well as the evangelical fervor appealed to African Americans. A proper balancing and blending of emotions and intellect was facilitated if the ritual was not totally "cold" and intellectually focused.

In spite of the plethora of Black denominations and congregations, there was and remains a continuum of diversity in worship styles within and between denominations, ranging from two extremes: emotional jubilance to solemn reverence. The early historical observations that denominational choices were made on the basis of educational level and color of skin are no longer accurate, nor are they fair. The stereotypes represented in this assumption began to dissolve during the civil rights movement.

Sociologists have delineated social scientific models for studying the African American Church that are helpful in looking at historical and current worship models.[14] Two models are especially helpful: (1) The "Ethnic Community-prophetic" model, developed by Anne Nelsen and Hart Nelsen, suggests that the Black church is a base for building a sense of ethnic identity and community interest among its members.[15] The time of corporate worship would be important in this process, with the preacher serving as a prophetic voice for the people. (2) The "Dialectical Model," developed by C. Eric Lincoln and Lawrence H. Mamiya, asserts that the church as an institution is involved in a constant series of dialectical tensions that shift between polarities throughout history.[16] The task of liturgical scholars, then, like that of social analysts, is to examine worship in the light of social conditions, in order to determine what its major orientation is in relation to dialectical polarities. Six major pairs of polarity dialectics are identified by these authors: priestly and prophetic; otherworldly versus this-worldly; universalism and particularism; communal and privatistic; charismatic versus bureaucratic; and resistance versus accommodation. The use of these models in studying African American worship traditions allows for a more dynamic view of worship along a continuum of tensions and struggles amid changes in society and the desire for liberation. This is especially important for music forms and styles that greatly affect worship.

Common Elements and Practices of Worship

All African American denominations (Protestants especially) can claim heritage in the Invisible Institution, regardless of when and where they enter denominational history. From extant evidence, we know that the early institutional churches and congregations first of all functioned in varying degrees in the "Ethnic Community-Prophetic" mode. Worshiping communities fluctuated on a continuum with respect to the aforementioned dialectics in their quest for racial ethnic identity and freedom. The extent to which major dialectical orientations occurred and lasted along the continuum during the early historical period depended on a number of factors: the geographical location of the congregation (urban, rural, north, south, east, or west), the number of "free" Blacks in the population, economic conditions of the community, job opportunities, educational opportunities, and size of the African American population in the community.

One pertinent factor that cannot be overlooked is the particular denominational *ethos* of the worshipers. Congregations that were part of a Euro-American denomination often attempted to follow the polity and procedures of the denomination, often discarding some of the traditional African American folkways. Where inherited orders of worship avoid references to songs other than hymns, psalms, and anthems, traditional Negro music (African American Spirituals) might be excluded. If the pastor is a seminary graduate, and a large number of members are college graduates, there might be a high frequency of the use of well-organized sermons, anthems, and anthem arrangements of Spirituals. If worshipers have been exposed to pipe organs, the membership is often willing to stretch its budget to purchase one. If "decency and order" in worship are encouraged by the parent church, any mode of worship contrary to this might be avoided. If "smells and bells" are part of worship in the parent church, one will experience these dimensions of denominational worship in the Black church. The use of vestments, paraments, liturgical colors, and preaching styles is often consistent with those that characterize the parent denomination. It should be noted, however, that Black denominations have also adopted many of the traditional Euro-American liturgical practices.

The denominational *ethos* is often affected and shaped by the geographical location, pastoral leadership, and daily life of worshipers.

Whereas one might identify a congregation by certain elements of worship, there might be a difference in congregational worshiping styles in Southern rural areas, for instance, where denominational interaction is intentional and frequent. Mobility across denominations is quite possibly the greater influencing factor for similarities in worship practices.

Most sensitive pastors are adept at adjusting services so that worshipers never lose the "common touch" and connection with their slave heritage. Dialectics and tensions between Euro-American denominational styles and the reality of the lived world have always been apparent. Some of the tension might have been caused by members of other denominations who looked on from the outside and assumed that the congregations were attempting to be white. Some tension is no doubt created by those in the congregation who might believe that the correct model for worship is that which is practiced in so-called "high churches." The dialectic nevertheless exists, and may indeed affect the growth *or* decline in membership.

There is regular and intentional interaction between congregations in many rural communities and small towns. A common historical practice that continues today is the exchanging of choirs and pastors between churches across denominations. Respected elderly persons are called upon to pray in worship services, regardless of denominational affiliation. Joint services of celebration were taking place, especially in rural areas, long before ecumenicism was "in vogue."[17] It is only natural that worship trends are similar, despite differences in denominational polity and theology. With the African kinship system still operating, many members across denominational lines are "very much at home" in any congregation. Church revivals and baptisms are adjusted to accommodate family and extended family from other churches. Whereas denominational differences in worship styles are acknowledged, styles of preaching, singing, and praying are often quite similar. This gives some indication of the continuation of styles from the Invisible Institution and Praise Houses as well as the free "borrowing" between denominations.

One of the factors that initially facilitated similarities in worship styles was the educational system. In segregated communities, churches often provided parochial schools for African Americans in which religious instruction and worship were part of the curriculum. When public schools were provided, daily worship continued, and teachers served as religious and moral leaders, utilizing not only Christian tenets, but also African American heroes and heroines as examples of those who had kept the faith. Among the heroes and heroines were preachers and leaders whose denominations were identified as an affirmation of denominational communal kinship. Although distinct theologies of worship were not taught, African American "ecumenical" styles of worship allowed students to experience a variety of practices.

There were entire communities and at least one township whose total population consisted of African Americans. One significant historical instance is Mound Bayou, Mississippi, an all-Black town, founded in 1887, where all Christians initially worshiped together outdoors in the town church, which was actually called the "Brush Arbor." Reminiscent of the Invisible Institution, services were literally held in the brush arbor, utilizing the elements of worship cited above.[18]

For Discussion

1. What are the basic reasons for the establishing of African American denominations?

2. Can any comparison be made between the sixteenth-century European Reformation led by Martin Luther and the need for African Americans to seek worship alternatives?

3. What are some unique features of African American worship?

4. What factors determine the differences in African American worship forms and styles?

How Music, Preaching, and Prayer Shape Contemporary African American Worship

African American congregations generally agree that corporate Christian worship is acknowledgment of and response to the presence and power of God as revealed in Jesus the Christ through the work of the Holy Spirit. Descriptive words often heard in response to the question of one's understanding of worship include *praise, adoration, reverence, thanksgiving, gratitude, celebration, penitence, submission,* and *commitment.* There are some who would include the Greek word *leitourgia* and explain that it is derived from *leiton* (pertaining to the people) and *ergon* (meaning "work" or "service"). Both corporate (or public) and personal (or private) worship are vital to the ongoing life of the church in general and the worshiping community in particular. Worship is basically person-centered—a creative encounter between God and persons. Nevertheless, personal worship is understood to be a necessary extension and continuation of corporate worship, rather than an isolated effort of an individual. God takes the initiative and calls the whole person to worship, rather than a mere portion of one's personhood.

God's call in Jesus Christ for corporate gatherings lends itself to a time when the community can claim and affirm kinship and mutual interdependence in a space where both social and spiritual hospitality are evident.[1] A common love bonding happens most effectively when verbal and nonverbal action can take place freely in a hospitable environment. It is the name of Jesus, spoken as an embodiment of love, that sets the hospitable climate for worship. In such a climate, worshipers can sing: "I'm so glad I'm here in Jesus' name!" Perhaps implied in the use of the personal pronoun "I" is the African understanding that I am (here) because we are, and we are here by the grace of God. Our presence in God's space frees us to be hospitable and open to welcome others. After all, the kindred of Jesus transcends natural (blood) ties of any human family, or those relationships that are already familiar (see Matt. 12:46-50; Mark 3:31-35; Luke 8:19-21). Worshipers are to reach out hospitably to those who may have "wandered" in, and to those who have come in obedience to God's will.

Traditionally, worship has not been a subject for discussion or theological discourse for African Americans. It is a divine experience, a dynamic happening, which in itself is a form of communication of obedience to God. As far as the records indicate, the first officially organized liturgical discussion among African Americans took place in 1986 at the Interdenominational Theological Center.[2] During the planning phase, and subsequently during the Consultations, a common, basic pattern of worship was noted, which transcends denominations and connects in many ways with worship in the Invisible Institution and Praise Houses. The pattern evolves out of certain psychological attitudes, emotions, and moods of worshipers. While the order that follows is not necessarily exact, an apparent dynamism and flow alternates between God's divine initiative and human responses.

> God's Divine Initiative (Call)
> Fellowship (Gathering)
> Adoration and Praise to God (Personal Testimonies)
> Penitence (Prayer)
> Hearing and Receiving the Word (Illumination)
> Renewal, Self-offering, and Dedication
> Service in the World (Mission)

While the pattern is in some ways similar to historic Euro-American worship patterns, the manner and style of the elements (acts) of worship that facilitate the flow are unique to the particular community of faith. A study of worship patterns among African peoples (in Africa and in diaspora) who are not thoroughly familiar with predetermined patterns of worship in other traditions has revealed the natural tendency of this flow to evolve. Confession of sin is more personal than corporate, except in denominations where this act of worship is included in ritual forms inherited (or continued) from Euro-American forms. Confessions are intricately bound in testimonies of personal conversion experiences.

Common Stylistic Elements (Acts) of Worship

Some of the elements of worship that evolved in the Invisible Institution and Praise House worship continue in dynamic forms in contemporary worship practices. There is also a trend toward recapturing traditional elements of African and African American spirituality in current practices. Thus the following common stylistic elements are identifiable as uniquely African American: music (vocal and instrumental), preaching, and praying.

Vocal Music: An Overview

The musical propensity of African Americans continues as perhaps the most visible conveyor of spirituality. Beginning with the original American folk music, the African American Spiritual, the religious music genre has included Black Gospel music (in its many forms and styles), Black meter hymns, as well as compositions by Black composers. The obvious African continuation of the inseparability of human life and nature, and the tendency toward total involvement of one's whole being in spiritual endeavors, necessitates a combining of forms and performance styles in a discussion of music.

The dialogical nature of worship, both vertical and horizontal, makes communication through music a major element of worship. Through the texts, singers can respond to God, comment on problems and joys, voice hope in the midst of despair, and assert their humanity. Because music is also rooted in the emotions, music can express the inexpressible and serve as a mask for realities of life. Even without extant records we know that Africans in diaspora made use of the musical gifts, which could not be chained by human bondage. They even continued the variety of uses of music, effectively blending sacred with secular, as they bonded and created new songs in a strange and alien land.

The importance of vocal music in worship is evidenced by the fact that one of the first published liturgical documents by and for African American worshipers was a hymnal. Richard Allen, founder of the African Methodist Episcopal Church (AMEC), prepared an assortment of books for his parishioners, one of which was a collection of hymns, which was published in two editions in 1801. The first, entitled *A*

Collection of Hymns and Spiritual Songs from Various Authors by Richard Allen, Minister of the African Methodist Episcopal Church, contained fifty-four hymns.[3] Ten additional hymns were added in the second edition, and a few changes were made in some texts of the original collection. Like other hymnal compilers of his day, Allen did not provide names of authors, appropriate tunes, or the source of hymns, so it is necessary to make a few speculative assumptions. Undoubtedly, some of the hymns were among his favorites that he had learned as an itinerant preacher on the Pennsylvania-Delaware circuit or in his service as an assistant preacher at Old George's Methodist Episcopal Church (Philadelphia). Some may have been taken from the commonly popular "oral" repertoire of African American worshipers. And others were apparently authored by Richard Allen.[4] Among the familiar hymnists are Isaac Watts, Charles Wesley, and John Newton.

In addition to its historic significance as the first "folk-selected" anthology of songs for African American worshipers, Allen's hymnal is the earliest source in history that attaches "wandering choruses" or "wandering refrains" to hymns.[5] This means that a short chorus or refrain is freely added to any standard hymn (at random). This improvisatory practice may have been in general use by African Americans as an extension of their oral folk method of contextualizing songs. It was also a means of retaining the informal environment of ritual action. Some of Allen's song texts were in the conventional "spiritual song" style of the Euro-American folk tradition. Others reflected his admonitions to improve the flock, and were directed toward the personal as well as group behavior of his congregation. His concern for emotional restraint and the "offensiveness" of unbridled emotions during worship is revealed in this song:

> Such groaning and shouting, it set me doubting,
> I fear such religion is only a dream;
> The preachers are stamping, the people are jumping,
> And screaming so loud that I neither could hear,
> Either praying or preaching, such horrible screaming,
> 'Twas truly offensive to all that were there.[6]

Two other early African American publishers of vocal music for worship were the Reverend Thomas Cooper (ca. 1775–ca. 1823) and William Wells Brown (1816–64). Cooper, a former slave who preached in the Northern United States, in England, and in Africa, was intentionally militant in his compositions. His 1820 hymnal, *The African Pilgrim's Hymns*, included 372 hymns, some of which he composed. Others were from hymnals in circulation at that time. His original compositions are often reminiscent of the more radical Spirituals that underscore the need to fight on.[7]

William Brown included texts of Spirituals composed and sung by slaves in his autobiography, *The Narrative of William W. Brown, a Fugitive Slave*, published in 1847. Some of the texts provide a historical description of the plight of Africans transported to America. These and similar songs that related historical events and lived experiences of their day were open to improvisation and re-creation, and provided impetus for emotional outlet for a people walking freely in God's story. Vocal expressions that began initially outside the worship setting continued in worship, providing the essential ingredients for the evolution of authentic worship music forms and styles. The historical progression of music for worship began with African utterances, chants, moans, and cries for deliverance as an enslaved people gradually accommodated the Christian faith. A progressive time line reveals overlapping vocal music traditions from African chants to twenty-first-century varieties of "contemporary music":

1619----1750----1800----1919----1950-----1960-----1980-----1990-----2001

African chants, etc.
                Spirituals--
                    Metered Music--
                    Improvised Hymns---
                            Traditional Gospel----------------------------
                                    Modern Gospel-------------------
                                        Contemporary Gospel----
                                        Gospel Hip-hop

Spirituals

It is difficult to establish an exact date for the origin of Spirituals as a musical genre. The earliest Spirituals emerged during the antebellum slave period and have been identified as the first authentic American folk song form. Spirituals were created both in and outside of the Christian worship environment. Some among the creators were, therefore, not oriented toward Christianity, whether in the hypocritical form taught or in what was being re-formed. Like other folk songs, Spirituals express the peculiar context, nature, experiences, values, and longings of the specific folk who created them. Inherent in the artistic outpouring of a people are linguistic complexities such as usage, purpose, and symbols. The preponderance of the use of personal pronouns in Spirituals can be attributed to a number of factors. The African understanding of one's personal interrelationship with others as all of the community experiences struggle is one factor. The "I" technically communicates that "we"—"all of us"—share in the struggle. There is also the possible intent of the singer to seek affirmation as a person of importance in an oppressive arena. John Lovell Jr. wisely observes that "a community of millions of people, each one recognized as important, produces a powerful folk effect."[8]

Whether in worship or at work, the earliest creators of Spirituals were part of a slave system. The persistent theme permeating the Spirituals is the need for radical change in the current social situation, which would mean freedom for the slave. For this reason, Spirituals can be classified generally as songs of protest. The appeal for deliverance is made to God, who delivers. The use of biblical stories and images, while not always expressive of orthodox Christian doctrine, provided a newly acquired religious referent to which African descendants skillfully fused their inherent primal world views. Texts of Spirituals reveal the slaves' confidence in the power of God in Jesus to render justice "on time."

The broad range of poetic literature gives evidence that religion and life are inextricably bound. A clear line of distinction can hardly be drawn between work songs, field hollers, blues, and songs about nature. To refer to the plethora of slave songs as *either* spiritual songs or secular songs is to misunderstand the community context and religious nature of the creators of the songs. Questions about the appropriateness of improvised Spirituals for worship beyond the Invisible Institution and the Praise House were a matter of controversy for both Euro-Americans and African Americans. Even Spirituals shaped during emotionally charged worship ("preaching Spirituals") could assume a different character in a work environment. New stanzas and the substitution of biblical words for words from the work-a-day world might have raised questions as to their appropriateness for continued use in worship. Questions of theology and the particular folk source of origin prevented Spirituals from finding a place in denominational hymnals until recently.

Spirituals have been used in African American worship continuously in some congregations, and more sporadically in others. There was a brief period of demise immediately following emancipation as African

Americans assumed a new status as freed people. A recovery of interest occurred following the popularization of Spirituals by the Fisk Jubilee choir in the late nineteenth century. Anthemized arrangements flourished at the turn of the century with the touring of Black college and university choirs. Congregations with college-trained pastors and choir directors perpetuated this genre as a choir form, often neglecting the folk style of congregational singing. Brief periods of decline in the use of the Spirituals in the twentieth century were caused by the rise of other more popular forms, such as Gospel music, quartets, soloists, and the use of Euro-American hymns in worship. The civil rights movement allowed an opportunity for renewed emphasis on the use of Spirituals as an important form of congregational music. The choice of Spirituals, the folk songs of a people whose freedom was not yet assured, was natural for Martin Luther King, Jr., in whose denominational tradition the "songs of Zion" had continued to be sung. The protest songs of antebellum slaves became protest songs, recalled and re-created for the twentieth-century freedom movement. The artistic gift of an African people proved to be a "timeless mirror" of the realities of society, and open to a continuing process of "becoming." Its origin in the folk community means that the creation of the Spiritual is never complete, and remains a means of community bonding.

A large number of Spirituals have been theologically indexed by topic and season of the Christian Year for use in worship. African Americans find these songs a source of inspiration and a natural means of responding to and communicating with the Almighty. Spirituals are a pastoral liturgical resource for any community of worshipers. Properly understood, Spirituals are the ageless psalms of a people in exile who poured out their praise, prayers, thanksgiving, and lament to God, in the midst of harsh struggles. They are analogous to theological documents, carefully and thoughtfully presented in simple and often symbolic language of a particular people.

Improvised Hymnic Forms

Extant texts and compilations authored by African Americans who lived during this period affirm the sacred/secular unity and the possible inclusion of popular texts and tunes that originated outside the church. In addition to religious songs composed in worship and at work and individually authored hymns, African Americans also incorporated

Euro-American hymns into their worship. Rather than retaining the Euro-American structure, hymns were reshaped or improvised in a folklike manner or "blackenized" as a means of contextualization. To sing hymns as they were heard in formalized settings did not lend itself to the social and spiritual bonding required of Africans in diaspora. The process of recreating and improvising hymns was a way of making the music their own.

Black Metered Music

Antebellum slaves were introduced to the somber and serious "lined-rote" method of psalm singing in religious and informal colonial gatherings. Religious instruction for the slaves included instruction in psalmody, which apparently appealed to the new converts. When African Americans were granted freedom to organize their own religious meetings, the singing of psalms was a requirement.[9] During the Great Awakening religious movement of the 1730s, the singing of hymns was popularized in the religious poetry of Isaac Watts. Psalm singing declined in favor of Watts's lively tunes and fresh texts.

The hymns of Isaac Watts appeared to have been favored perhaps because of the straightforwardness and simplicity of texts and music. A special style of "metered hymn singing," beginning with, but not limited to, hymns by Watts, was influenced by the a cappella "call-and-response" technique employed both in Spirituals and in the "lining tradition" of early Euro-Americans. The procedure consists of the chanting or "tuning" of one or two lines of text in "singsong" or recitative (*Sprechgesang*) fashion by a precentor, deacon, preacher, or song leader, ending on a definite pitch. The congregation "surges in," often before the line is completed, and sings the same line with some elaboration of the tune. It is the song leader's task not only to set the pitch, but also to project loudly, clearly, and enthusiastically enough so as to encourage full participation by the congregation. Melodies are inevitably altered and shaped according to the needs of the community. The semblance of an "exact" melody preserved in the memories of song leaders and transmitted by the oral tradition often defies exact musical scoring. Supporting harmonies of parallel thirds, fourths, fifths, and sixths are added according to artistic "ears" and musical preferences of the gathered community.

The printed score with meter signatures and structured rhythms of the original hymn is meaningless in this unaccompanied vocal art form. Additionally, the technical designations of common meter (6.8.6.8.), long meter (8.8.8.8.), and short meter (6.6.8.6.) have nothing to do with the description of Black metered music. The term *meter* is merely borrowed from the music vocabulary to describe a newly shaped folk-form originating with hymns by Isaac Watts, which are referred to as "Dr. Watts."

The spiritual and emotional impact of this style of singing in African American worship is indescribable. Although this style of singing in Euro-American churches was discouraged and supplanted by the "proper way of singing" taught in singing schools, the tradition of lining hymns continued with fervor among Black worshipers. It is not unusual to find the integration of metered music and Spirituals. Metered hymn singing in African American worship, dating from the early nineteenth century (ca. 1807 or 1810), continues today. It is employed most often by Black Baptists in Southern rural communities, along with other forms that reflect the constantly expanding repertoire of music forms and styles in worship.

Other Improvised Hymns

As the growth of African American denominations and congregations accelerated, and literacy increased, worshipers borrowed hymns freely from other traditions. In the socialization process, hymns were adapted in a variety of ways, and remain open to further shaping as congregational situations dictate. Original texts are often retained, but the musical performance style of the "anti-structured" worshiping context provides the unique "blackenized" identity. In reference to improvised hymns, Wyatt Tee Walker observes that

> the oral tradition introduces itself again; the "standard," or well known, Euro-American hymns require no special instruction for Black rendition. The Black religious community instinctively knows how to sing them. The mode of singing is common to the Black religious experience and is passed from one generation to another via an oral tradition in Black sacred music.[10]

Current improvisational performance styles often include stylized instrumental accompaniment that enhances the emotional import. Improvisations may express the community's exuberant joy, contemplation, or a combination of both simultaneously. The pastor, song leader, and other worshipers are free to inject "lead-in" phrases or brief lines of testimony to personalize certain stanzas. Congregational affirmations of personal "additions" also indicate social identity with individual needs.

Hymnals Compiled by African Americans

Hymnals published by African Americans for use as an important liturgical resource in worship began in 1801 through the efforts of Richard Allen, founder of the AME Church.

The first official AMEC denominational hymnal was the 1818 (words only) edition, published two years after the 1816 AMEC Inaugural Conference. Few changes were made in subsequent editions of the 314 hymns and Spirituals published between 1818 and 1872. The first revised hymnal, containing 1,115 hymns, chants, and doxologies, published in 1876, was the authorized hymnal until 1892. Two more editions with words only were published before the 1898 hymnal, the first published with words and music. Hymnals published in 1941 and 1954 did not include as many Spirituals and hymns by Black composers as does the 1984 *Bicentennial Hymnal*.

First editions of hymnals by other Black denominations include the Union African Church in 1822; the African Methodist Episcopal Zion Church in 1839 (the 1957 hymnal is acknowledged as the first "original" hymnal produced by the AMEZ Church); Christian Methodist Episcopal Church, 1891; the Church of Christ (Holiness) in 1899; National Baptist, 1903; National Baptist, USA, 1924; Progressive Baptist in 1976; and the Church of God in Christ (Pentecostal) in 1982.[11]

Although it was not an official denominational hymnal, Marshall V. Taylor compiled and published a hymnal for use by Black congregations of the Methodist Episcopal Church in 1883. Charles A. Tindley, a Black Methodist Episcopal pastor, began to publish collections of his songs in 1905. Other significant hymnal compilations by African Americans that have influenced the music of worship include *National Jubilee Melodies*, circa 1916 (Baptist); *The Gospel Pearls* (Baptist), 1921; *The New National Baptist Hymnal*, 1977; *Lift Every Voice* (Episcopal), 1981; *Songs of Zion* (United Methodist), 1981; and *Lead Me, Guide Me* (Catholic), 1987.

In acknowledgment of the contributions of racial ethnics to music for worship, the official hymnals published by The Christian Reformed Church in 1988, The United Methodist Church in 1989, and The Presbyterian Church (USA) in 1990 include a significant amount of music from the African American experience. In this way cultural offerings are shared with entire denominations, and represent a composite of ecumenical hymnody.

Black Gospel Music

Traditional Gospel

Black Gospel music refers to both a genre (song form) of musical composition and a vocal or instrumental performance style. Both represent a composite of a variety of musical expressions: Spirituals, metered hymns, improvised hymns, blues, ragtime, jazz, and nineteenth-century Euro-American gospel hymns. The folksy earthiness that distinguishes Black Gospel from other musical genres recalls primal empathetic features that are different from Euro-American aesthetics. For the African American, the aesthetic is integrally bound with feelings and emotions that allow the "beautiful" to emerge from the soul.

Gospel music as a performance style makes it possible to "gospelize" any form of music. In the tradition of improvised hymns, congregations are prone to alter a hymn, song, Spiritual, or anthem to suit the musical tastes of the particular community. In Gospel music, however, the attention is usually focused on individual performers. A choir or the congregation is expected to support and participate with the soloist, and the community can be unified by the leadership of a skilled, spirit-filled singer.

Thomas A. Dorsey, an African American musician, was first to apply the name "Gospel" to this twentieth-century urban-Spiritual form and style. In a personal interview, Dorsey affirms that he did not *coin* the phrase *gospel music*. He simply took an existing concept and merged it with his blues performance practices.[12] Dorsey, a talented blues and jazz musician, was influenced by the style of the religious compositions of Charles A. Tindley, a Black Methodist pastor. Dorsey's texts, as well as those of subsequent Gospel musicians, are commentaries on personal religious experiences in a society that is most often hostile. Tony Heilbut writes of the language of Black Gospel songs:

> Lyrics may sound banal, but they talk about the things that matter most to poor people. . . . A poor [person's] concerns are . . . staying alive . . . healthy . . . and financially solvent. Combine these pressing demands

with a diction made up of the most vivid idioms and some of the most old-fashioned imagery, and the gospel language begins to make sense.[13]

Dorsey was a pioneer in fusing instrumental accompaniments clearly associated with forms created outside the church. Keyboard accompaniments are most often quite rhythmic, "bluesy," highly syncopated, and intricately necessary as a vehicle of support for properly communicating the message of the text. Because the Black Gospel music style is so similar to music characterized as "secular," there is a constant interaction and mutual feeding of styles. Gospel music has also found a home on performance stages and in night clubs, and thrives to some extent on the impetus and momentum gained from applause and accolades of the "audience." Back home in worship, Gospel music evokes heightened expectations of secular/sacred fervor, which permeates the congregation. In both "worlds" the community is bonded as it participates with musicians without constraints.

General vocal characteristics that give Gospel music its distinct flavor are vocal agility, tone color, and an extensive vocal range. Vocal timbres of the best Gospel singers range from well-modulated "straight tones" to strained, full-throated growls and shrills, with lots of controllable vibrato. Melodies are "best" executed if the leader can improvise with spontaneous interpolations, ornamentations, bends, and portamentos (scoops and slides). The use of the falsetto voice has enhanced Gospel music since the 1960s, adding a new dimension to other features that have popularized this genre. The tempo is left most often to the discretion of the leader. Slower tempos are subject to elaborate vocal embellishments. Faster tempos lend themselves to rhythms that are more syncopated. The repetition of words and phrases, in combination with other musical devices, helps create an emotional impact on both the singers (leader and choir) and the congregation.

Modern and Contemporary Gospel Music

Societal conditions of worshipers, along with technological advancements and new musical inventions, have created new possibilities for the evolution of Gospel forms and styles. The civil rights movement deepened the awareness of societal inequities, and attention was focused again on the "beloved community," which could be brought together through music. The electric organ, with its vibrato capabilities, and microphones that had invaded the worship space expanded the quality of sound, style, and mechanics of delivery.

The term *modern* is generally applied to Gospel songs that emerged in the 1960s and continue to overlap with newly evolving forms. Occurring on the heels of the 1957 Newport Jazz Festival, where traditional Gospel music was featured, the sacred Gospel sound became an acceptable worldly sound. Gospel music soon "hit the charts" as a popular sound, and there was little if any distinction between Gospel music for worship or for entertainment.

Black worship was affected by this new phenomenon, not only because of the "show dimension," but because of the societal context. Racial tensions were eased as people resorted to achieving freedom and bonding through music. The latest Gospel "hit" often became the special music for worship, if it could be learned from the record fast enough. Large, elaborately robed "stage" choirs, popularized by the Edwin Hawkins singers, became the models for church choirs. A new "rock" permeated worship, with lots of hand clapping, keyboard accompaniment, and trap drum sets to help make a joyful noise unto the Lord!

Contemporary Gospel music (which emerged during the 1980s) supplements other sounds heard in some Black worship services. The religious texts are often supported by chordal harmonies that have not been the traditional musical support for religious texts. Youth are finding worship more meaningful because they can identify with sounds from their own context. The contention is that the work of God's people in worship (*leitourgia*) should not be limited to ritual action that is not contextualized.

Preaching

"Is there a word from the Lord?" This question, which was imbedded in the souls of the slaves, continues with African American worshipers. For some, all of the other elements are preliminary to the preached word. This confirms the importance and centrality of preaching in Black worship from the Invisible Institution to the present. Worshipers come prepared to hear the good news delivered by inspired preachers whose reputations often encourage attendance at worship. Those who worship with openness find the divine activity of God in the sermon of a female or male messenger of God, who has accepted his or her call and claimed the authority to preach with power.

The preached word, presented so that it is heard and experienced, allows one to know that "there *is* a way out of no way," and frees worshipers to celebrate this fact with the preacher. The word from the Lord is heard with the ears of one's total being, and it is experienced in the poetic flow of the preacher. The word elicits holistic responses that may begin in the gathered community, and will continue with worshipers as they move into the world.[14]

Whereas currently a variety of preaching styles is utilized in Black worship, the traditional perception is that the preacher is able to "tell the story" (literally communicate) in language, symbols, and symbolic mannerisms that speak directly to the needs of worshipers. The messenger brings to the task a variety of gifts: knowledge of the Word, a divine listening ear, and a "feel" for the gathered community. With these gifts, the preacher serves as a divine conduit through which the fresh Word of God can flow without encumbrance.

With a basic acknowledgment that the cultural context of worshipers is a determining factor in modes of ritual action, preaching in the Black church can also be viewed as a poetic cultural art form.[15] While authentically biblically based, the messages live and breathe with the community. Through the use of descriptive imagery and tonal and word paintings, stories come to life in the imagination of worshipers, so that hope is portrayed in the bleakest of circumstances. Dialogical communication skillfully takes place between preacher and the community, thus both must listen ardently to the other. This verbal call-and-response African form can easily evolve into a musical dialogue, sometimes with the aid of a skilled organist or pianist.

Some preachers continue the tradition of a symphonically orchestrated form of sermonizing. One can wait in anticipation of an *adagio* movement, which could gradually build up to a *scherzo* celebration, or a *sonata allegro* form with numerous recapitulations and a lengthy *coda*. An artistic form of occasional pauses during the sermon, especially during the time of celebration, helps capture the experiencing attention of worshipers. Along with the participatory dialogue, which often heightens emotions, worshipers are listening for and receive a fresh word from the Lord. Even amid more emotional styles, the preaching may be didactic or proclamatory. In all instances, the preacher is aware of the urgent need of the community to deepen its faith and spiritual life.

Just as with other elements of worship, so also one can expect that preaching in the Black church is not the same in every service of worship. Some worshiping contexts may dictate a less emotionally involved form of communication because of varying needs rather than as an attempt to imitate any other worshiping community. With the increasing acceptance of the ordination of women as clergy, the community can anxiously anticipate new forms of Black preaching. "New occasions teach new duties," and may demand new and different styles, which will in no way negate the traditional preaching heritage. As a folk art form, divinely inspired by God in Jesus Christ, Black preaching, too, is always in "process of becoming."

Prayer

> Here I stand, Lord, like an empty pitcher before a full fountain, just waiting to be filled. . . . Thank you for allowing me to wake up with the blood still running warm in my veins.[16]

The prayer tradition of contemporary Black worship, like music and preaching, rooted in Africa, has been nurtured in meeting houses and in the personal prayer lives of slaves and remains a means of vital force for spiritual release and fulfillment. It has continued in some current African American worship services without interruption. The familiar metaphoric prayer language, shaped by the common suffering of African Americans and transmitted by the oral tradition, continues in many services of worship. The attitude of reverence that pray-ers mysteriously assume makes one aware of the depth of faith and the dynamics of a personal relationship with the Divine. One can "have a little talk with Jesus" and know that everything will be all right. Pray-ers still claim to be "empty pitchers," open for divine empowerment, not only to enter the space of the divine prayer altar, but to be able to say what really needs to be said.

A spontaneous offering of prayers is understood to be evidence that God initiates and carries the prayer forth. With this observation, however, one finds similar phrases and metaphors that are common in every denomination, which speaks to the powerful gift of memory. Even the sequential ordering of elements in prayers (from thanksgiving to submission), and the unlimited amount of time that one can take to pray will be the same or quite similar. Although spontaneously offered, there is evidence of a memorized body of materials from traditional Black prayers. Common expressions reveal a strong sense of spiritual oneness and comfort in the gathered community where strength and security can be found. The ability to recall biblical passages and concepts, carried over from traditional Black prayer, is one of the measures of the depth of spirituality of prayer leaders.

Prayers printed in the bulletin to be prayed (or read) together by the congregation have little appeal to many Black worshipers. This limits the possibility of spontaneity and for some lacks the natural approach to God under the power of the Spirit. Operative here is the understanding that one called upon to pray must yield to the power of God, who speaks with the folks directly when they close their eyes, open their mouths, and rely on the enabling power of the Spirit to fill them. To read or pray words that are written, no matter how carefully they reflect another's spiritual direction, is to interfere with the natural form of communication between the divine and humanity.

It is not unusual in worship for prayer leaders to "tune" their prayers in the same manner as preachers, as the Spirit leads. This, too, is a continuation of the oral tradition in which natural vocal inflections are "ornamented" with bends, twists, and quavers, providing a musical flow. This style frees the community for an indwelling of the Spirit and invites similar musical responses from the congregation, so that the entire church is "singing the prayer." Where congregations are free and uninhibited, someone will "raise a song" that picks up themes from the prayer, thereby reshaping the ordering of elements.

One of the most difficult assignments for theological students is to prepare various forms of prayers in writing. One student insisted the entire semester that he could not write prayer language on paper. It was necessary for him to tape-record his prayers for class submission, so that we were able to verbally discuss matters of concern. After calling to his attention his tendency to alternately punctuate every sentence with "Thank you, Jesus," and "O Lord God," he was able to determine the need to listen to himself pray aloud and on paper.

Prayer continues to be a basic form through which African American worshipers express their faith as they seek wholeness and affirmation for personhood. As a communal form, it provides affirmation, hope, and healing for all gathered, and the opportunity for intercession for those who are not in attendance. Even with printed bulletins, prayers in the order of service may not be limited to the form assigned. Invocations might include self-dedication and pastoral concerns. Most, if not all, prayers include words of thanksgiving, pleas for help and remembrance, and willingness to submit to the will of God. Prayers, especially of the laity, may be addressed interchangeably to either person of the God Head.

The close affinity with the divine and earthly Jesus is also apparent in prayers. The name of Jesus punctuates much of the prayer language.

Special "prayer and praise" times that establish the momentum for worship have continued without interruption from the Invisible Institution and Praise Houses in some congregations, particularly Baptists. Special times for prayer have been reinstituted recently as part of the recovery of the Black tradition. Common prayer time during the time of gathering for worship includes Sunday morning and revival devotional services. Leadership is historically provided by deacons, which in some denominations is an office held only by men. Women have historically assumed this role in Pentecostal churches, with a recent trend toward the inclusion of women as leaders in other denominations. A time for prayer and praise during worship in some Black denominations preceded the current trend popularized by television. The period designated as the "altar call" meets the needs of worshipers who are seeking special prayers, healings, or blessings. Some come to the "altar" to offer themselves in renewal for Christian discipleship. Even congregations that may not theologically claim a special, ongoing altar space might extend a call for those with needs listed above. The historic "mourners' bench," where persons seeking an encounter with God are aided by the community to come to that point, or "come through," is not as prevalent as in previous years. One might find such a point of prayer as an element of worship in Southern, rural areas, especially during revivals. Other special times for prayer common among many Black worshipers include weekly prayer meetings, prayer bands, and prayer time during civil rights rallies.

Inherent in the ongoing discovery and recovery of the Black prayer tradition is a natural, childlike, holy boldness to approach the throne of grace. This boldness is founded on an unwavering trust in the promises of God, which allows the community to unashamedly express its faith. One approaches God boldly, and yet stands as an empty pitcher before a full fountain. Open and vulnerable before the Divine, one is free to accept the in-filling power from a God who, in the words of a traditional African American prayer, "sits high and looks low . . . snatched our soul from the gates of hell, and put a new song and prayer in our hearts."

Diversity of Responses

African Americans are not all alike! Nor are all worship practices the same. There are individual histories, just as there are denominational histories, that share similarities and yet affirm the right to be unique. Although there are numerous ways to determine differing worship gifts, the approach used here is the basic matter of theology and doctrine that helped shape current worship patterns. The assumption here is that in some ways what is believed in doctrine helps determine how a congregation will worship.[17] Unfortunately, the lack of documentation of theologies and practices of worship by African American churches will limit a detailed discussion from a denominational perspective.

Methodist Traditions

African American Methodists claim in varying degrees the theological heritage of John Wesley with the American shaping by Bishop Francis Asbury. The uninhibited enthusiasm in the worship of early Methodists appealed to people of African descent in America. Equally appealing was the Methodist piety, which was supported and encouraged in worship and through spiritual discipline. Small class meetings were helpful in shaping spiritual directions and discipline, and in promoting corporate prayer. Rituals were not complicated by the use of service books by a community of faith that was just beginning to read.

Forms of worship are similar to the parent Methodist body, but styles of action are culturally and contextually determined. Two sacraments, the Lord's Supper and baptism, are observed in each of the Black Methodist denominations, with rituals adapted from The (Euro-American) Methodist Church.

African Methodist Episcopal Church

Richard Allen initially modified the Methodist form of worship to accommodate the culture and aesthetics of the new African American congregation. The services naturally assumed the character of worship in the slave community. With the exposure of some of the leaders to other worship modes, conflicts arose as to what forms and styles of music were appropriate for worship. AME Bishop Daniel A. Payne made the first change toward what he said would be "improvement" by replacing the practice of lining-out hymns with choral music sung by choirs between 1841 and 1842.[18] Payne further opposed the notion of an African American ideology and encouraged churches to pattern worship after the Euro-American Methodist counterpart. In spite of his efforts, most AME churches, especially in the South, adapted the basic worship structure inherited from the Methodists to include styles from the slave heritage.

In time, an AMEC worship ethos developed that is best understood and appreciated from experience. There is a strong emphasis on preaching, prayer, fellowship, and a diversity of forms and styles of music. Unique elements in the order of service are the use of the doxology at the beginning and the end of the service, and the use of the Decalogue (long form or abridged). There are several ritual options for the Lord's Supper, one of which includes sung Amens, chants (including the Lord's Prayer), and one stanza of "Nearer My God to Thee." A book of services prepared for the bicentennial not only makes available all rituals of the Church, but contains other liturgical information for laypersons and clergy.[19]

African Methodist Episcopal Zion Church

The AMEZ Church originated in New York and has its largest membership east of the Mississippi, with concentration in North Carolina. Out of Methodist Episcopal doctrinal roots, the Church has shaped its own theology, acknowledging the Good News in Jesus Christ amid the realities of the marginal existence of its membership. Key terms of the Christian faith, such as *salvation, freedom, Kingdom of God, sin,* and *atonement* have different meanings from those of Euro-Americans. The Apostles' Creed is the only formal creed of the denomination. The discipline of the Church, articles of religion, and constitutional requirements are the same as those of the Methodist Episcopal heritage.[20]

The order of worship, although similar to the Methodist Episcopal Church from which it separated in 1796, is different in terms of style and action. Preaching, prayer, fellowship, and music in worship show evidence of strongly family-oriented worship.

Christian Methodist Episcopal Church

The CME Church is the only Black Methodist denomination that was organized with the cooperation and support of its parent body, the Methodist Episcopal Church, South. The first bishops elected by the Church were ordained under the auspices of the MEC, South, and all separate properties used for slave members were authorized to be deeded to the newly organized CME Church. Its membership is nationwide and heavily concentrated in the Southeast. The doctrines are the same as those of the Methodist Episcopal Church, but practical application reflects special concern for social justice and inclusiveness. The Apostles' Creed and the Nicene Creed provide their creedal expression.

Foundations for CME worship, an explanation of each of the elements of worship, an outline of the Christian Year, and liturgical colors are included in the *Book of Rituals and Aids to Worship* (1987). In the introduction of this document is the claim that worship is an acknowledgment that God is not far from any one of us, and that God in Jesus Christ is worthy of worship whether in services of corporate worship or in acts of secular work. The emphasis in the *Book of Rituals* is on corporate worship, or what some Black Christians call "The Meeting"—the gathering of two or three in the name of Jesus. Elements specifically highlighted in the introduction are singing the songs of Zion, preaching the gospel, and the occasional celebration of the sacrament of Holy Communion. The pattern of worship is outlined in six steps: vision of God, adoration and praise, confession of sin, pardon, challenge (through the preached word), and decision.

Baptists

Black Baptist churches were initially related to Euro-American denominations. Emergence into independent bodies resulted from protest against restrictions and unequal treatment by parent bodies, rather than doctrinal differences. Many Black Baptists were connected to Euro-American organizational structures through the African Baptist Missionary Society, a division that devoted most of its work to mission efforts in Africa. Separation from these structures was facilitated by virtue of the autonomous Baptist polity. Unlike their Euro-American counterparts, the Church has been and remains a center for political activities for the community. The concerns are not only for Baptists, but for all who suffer injustice.

Baptists are united on the basic principle of theological individualism, a belief that the individual is able to interpret the will of God for himself or herself. The individual is responsible for determining biblical truths in communion with God and fellowship with Jesus the Christ.

Authority over a local church is housed within the congregation itself. It is not unusual for factions to develop within congregations when there are disagreements on basic theological issues, and splits are likely to occur.

One of the most significant doctrines is the autonomy of the local church. Orders of worship among Black Baptists are diverse, reflecting their autonomous nature. The contents of worship range from a basically simple outline of elements (especially in rural areas) to a more detailed outline. Worship often begins with a "devotional period," followed by a prelude and call to "formal" worship. In most instances, there is an abundance of music and prayers, which builds to and culminates in preaching and an invitation to discipleship (opening of the doors of the church) at the end.

Baptism and the Lord's Supper are understood to be ordinances rather than sacraments in the Baptist Church. At the heart of the doctrine is "believers' baptism" by immersion. This restricts baptism to persons who are old enough to make a personal profession of faith after a decisive experience of faith and repentance. It also means that persons baptized by other modes, or as infants, generally must be rebaptized if they choose to hold membership in a Baptist church. However, with a doctrine of autonomy, some Baptists now accept previous baptisms, if they occurred upon a confession of faith.

The Lord's Supper is understood to be a memorial meal that lends itself to fresh encounters between Christ and his people. Various meanings are applied, but most Black Baptists understand that this is not a "mere" memorial pointing back to ancient history. It is a visible symbol that reinforces the gospel preached in words that remind worshipers of all the events in the life of Christ. The local congregation determines whether the Table will be "fenced" or open to other believers.

Pentecostal and Holiness

With so many varieties of Pentecostal and Holiness churches with local authority, it is difficult to generalize about worship in these traditions. The Holiness movement began first as a reform movement in Methodism in 1867 when a group of Methodists organized the "National Camp Meeting Association for the Promotion of Holiness" (later called National Holiness Association). Aspects of Wesley's theology with emphasis on the importance of sanctification or Christian perfection appealed especially to Methodists and Baptists. Initial leadership in the movement and the ultimate shaping of worship practices included African Americans and Euro-Americans, males and females.

With the evolution of the movement into formal structures of denominations and sects, some worshipers added features of Pentecostalism: baptism of the Holy Spirit as evidenced by speaking in tongues and spiritual healing. The great Pentecostal explosion during the Azusa Street revivals in 1906, led by William J. Seymour, a Black preacher, marked the beginning of the worldwide spread of this movement. One of the significant characteristics of Pentecostal worship is its openness to the inclusion of a variety of racial groups at every level of society. People are valued and affirmed in worship for the gifts from God that they bring and offer for the good of the whole.

The Church of God in Christ

The origin of the Church of God in Christ (COGIC) stems from these revivals. The initial movement that led to the formation of the Church began in and around Lexington, Mississippi, under the leadership of Charles Harrison Mason. The first general assembly and official founding date of the Church in 1907 distinguishes it as the sole incorporated Pentecostal body in existence from 1907 to 1914. As such, the COGIC denomination was the only ecclesiastical authority to which Euro-American Pentecostal churches could appeal for the ordination of ministers. Over a period of time a large number of Pentecostal churches evolved and shaped their own ecclesiastical structure and worship practices.

The *Official Manual* of the Church of God in Christ, published in 1973, includes Articles of Religion upon which worship is doctrinally based. Ordinances of the Church include baptism, the Lord's Supper, and foot washing. Baptism is the rite by which persons who profess faith are admitted to the Lord's Table. The Zwinglian, or memorial, view undergirds the Lord's Supper. As baptized believers partake of the meal, they enter by faith into a spiritual union with Christ in memory of the Lord's suffering and death on the cross. This act of faith also symbolizes the union of believers with one another as new life, strength, and joy are given to the soul. The regularity of the meal is left to the discretion of the pastor in charge of the congregation.

Foot washing, when observed, is held subsequent to the Lord's Supper, with women and men separated for the ordinance. The focus on humility and servanthood is powerfully expressed in the act itself, and in the joyous singing of the congregation, which accompanies the rite.

A detailed ordering of worship elements for each of the ordinances, burials, marriage, the renewal of marriage vows, and special services is included in the *Manual*, but there is no suggested order for regular Sunday worship.[21] Distinguishing features are not so much in *what* is done, but *how* it is done. A deeply spiritual aura permeates the worship environment during periods of testimony, exuberant singing, praying, preaching, healing, shouting, conversions, and offertory. Each of the elements is accompanied by a variety of keyboard and percussion instruments. The entire service is so musical that keyboard accompaniment of the preacher's tonal message does not appear out of the ordinary even to worshipers who are not familiar with this particular style. One is made aware of the importance of the keyboard for helping the preacher "stay on pitch" in the heightened moments of celebration. The length of time for worship is determined by the spiritual momentum engendered by each of the elements. A service may last two or three hours, and the fellowship afterward could prolong it another hour.

Mixing and Merging Elements

The unique gifts and contributions of African Americans to the American liturgical heritage often escape the pen of Euro-American writers. One reason for the neglect of positive references is perhaps embodied in John F. Watson's negative observation in 1819, at which time he chastised white Methodist worshipers for engaging in singing practices similar to the "illiterate blacks of the society."[22] His opinion that African Americans were illiterate and, therefore, incapable of contributing to the enhancement of worship was no doubt the prevalent attitude among Euro-Americans.

A more positive note was struck by Daniel Mathews 158 years later. According to his account, white evangelicals were more receptive to the participation of African Americans in worship. Although this openness conveys a concern that surpassed the actual feelings of Euro-Americans, evangelical worship was emotionally more appealing to African Americans. The involvement of Blacks in worship contributed significantly to

American evangelical history. Mathews contends that "precisely because of that common public worship and because neither people could free itself of the other, the two religious modes . . . black and white—cannot be understood apart from each other."[23]

Mathews is clear that Blacks and whites did not share identical religious experiences and ultimate hopes, but that worship and social involvement were mutually affected by the other. He affirms that "the religious ethos which [Southern] blacks projected into society was rich and powerful precisely because it was something which blacks had fashioned for themselves and in doing so revealed a new way of expressing Christianity."[24]

There is not sufficient evidence or agreement as to specific elements transferred from one racial group to another. Where there are similarities in styles of responses, origins can be traced both to Africa and to Europe. For Euro-Americans, various forms of emotional ecstasy, a joyous sense of release and celebration, and psychological transformations during conversion experiences were universal phenomena of revivals in England, Wales, Ireland, New England, and colonies in the South. These responses were also characteristic of the worship of African peoples. Contrary to the opinion of white observers of the eighteenth and nineteenth centuries, Blacks were not "merely imitating emotional white worshipers." Vitality and emotional fervor in preaching, conversion, congregational responses, and enthusiastic singing were perhaps more African than Euro-American. The incantational preaching style of white Baptists and Methodists was similar to the interaction between leader and worshipers in African traditional religions. The use of water in rites of passage (referred to as baptism by Euro-Americans) was also familiar to African converts.

Although needs, images, symbols, and experiences differed, it is possible that the similar style of liturgical behavior provided a means of religious contact between the two races. This form of contact, where barriers of race are transcended in worship (often just for the worshiping moment) apparently facilitated the involvement of Blacks with whites in the founding of Pentecostal movements in the nineteenth and early twentieth centuries. Current Pentecostal and nondenominational movements also involve interaction between the races, indicating that the trend continues. Common behavioral practices that continue in separate places of worship may indicate a fusion or adaptation of elements rather than an expropriation, in toto, by either group.

African American Congregations in Euro-American Churches

The theology and polity of each of the Euro-American denominations with an African American constituency basically undergirds the worship order. Local congregations have either continued the African American styles or have recovered this rich heritage in worship in recent years. Along with the inclusion of Spirituals and songs reflective of the African American heritage in hymnody, some of the denominations are intentional in the inclusion of some of the liturgical heritage in denominational liturgical resources.

For Discussion

1. Is it important to you that the gathered community is a hospitable community? Why?

2. How often are songs from the African American tradition incorporated in your regular worship experiences?

3. Examine your denomination's hymnal to determine the number of Spirituals and other songs from the African American tradition that are included.

4. What are some ways that spontaneous prayers and responses might be included in services of worship that normally do not lend themselves to spontaneity?

5. Is it possible for worship to be so free-flowing that a call for things to be done "decently and in order" becomes necessary? How are spontaneity and planned responses carefully balanced in worship?

WORSHIP AS EMPOWERMENT

T he concept of empowerment for the gathered and scattered church is rooted in New Testament references to power as the divine ability to continue the work of Christ. The Greek term *exousia* best expresses the concept of the unlimitedness, unrestrictedness, and sovereignty of God, whose very Word is power. The general use of *exousia* in the New Testament denotes the absolute possibility of being and acting, founded in God alone, the absolute source of all power and legality. God's power given to Jesus allows him to empower his disciples and subsequently the church. The power promised before Christ's ascension (Acts 2:1-4) is a gift from God—a gift that frees the individual and community to the possibility of being and acting according to the will of God alone (Luke 12:5; Acts 1:7; Jude 25; Rom. 9:21). Power, divinely given, denotes freedom with responsibility (Mark 13:34; 1 Cor. 9:1ff.). Empowerment enables one to be all that God wants one to be and to do what is divinely fitting and edifying.

A community of faith that receives strength from God's saving power, epitomized in the power of Christ's resurrection, can face perils and endure struggles because of the knowledge and experience of the protective power of God. Christian worship begins, receives impetus, and continues with God's divine intervention and empowerment. Under the power of the Holy Spirit, worshipers assemble in response to God's call. The Word of God has power to speak to the whole person and the entire community, taking account of personal feelings, perceptions, and the realities of human experiences. The assembly listens and responds to the timeless story of the mysterious power of God in Jesus the Christ.

For Africans in America, God's divine intervention began prior to the experiences of a harsh slave system. God had been actively present in the lives of African peoples long before their forced move to the colonies. In a variety of ways, primal world views, basic beliefs, and ways of knowing God from affective and cognitive experiences became the foundation for empowerment in worship in assembly and empowerment for survival in life. The undergirding religious nature of Africans has provided, as Gayraud Wilmore observes, "an essential thread in the fabric of Black culture," which transcends regional differences and socioeconomic backgrounds.[1]

Evidence of the strength of that binding thread is the continual authentic expression of personal and corporate praise to God in Jesus the Christ in worship. Patterns of worship woven over the years, from slavery to the present age, provide a tapestry of styles that empower and liberate African Americans to act responsibly in a world that seeks to limit power to a few. The ground of religious consciousness inherent in African traditions provides an awareness that the ultimate power emanates from and is owed to a "Holy Other." God's empowerment and liberation of people reflect a God who will "always be God." This is expressed in a slave song of African roots, "God Don't Never Change." Celebrations of the acts of God in history reflect the hope that is made possible through God incarnate in Jesus, who opened the way for a socially powerless people to claim the walk in God's story. In Jesus the Christ, God entered the "givenness of a world" besieged with evil powers, walked, talked, and ate with the powerless as well as those in power, and accepted the vulnerability of the cross. Suffering and dying at the hands of the socially powerful, God in Jesus yielded to a divine demonstration of victory over all powers in the resurrection and ascension. Saving acts of God reveal the promise of a future that, as Ivan Illich reminds us, "has already broken into the present."[2]

The warp and woof of African American worship is a celebration of the reality of a transformed relationship between Creator and creature. This relationship undergirds the empowerment that is expressed in freedom by the grace of God. It is no wonder, then, that thanksgiving is so prominent in nearly all elements of worship. Prayers, testimonies, and songs of praise offered at the beginning of worship include thanks for the power of God, which enables individuals and the community to "wake up this morning with blood still running warm in our veins." Without this, the community would not be able to respond in praise for all that God is, has been, and will be.

Historical Foundations of Empowerment

It is important to remain in touch with the history of African American worship. Africans in America, in the beginning, were willing to risk severe punishment and even their lives to exercise the "freedom" to experience the newness of life in Jesus Christ. Empowered to transcend the laws of bondage, slaves continued the old ways of African traditional religions, claimed the old ways of Judeo-Christianity, and transformed both into something new. Under the power of the Holy Spirit, the perception of the sacred/secular unity of life continues to allow corporate worship, *koinonia*, to continue in the scattered community, *diakonia*. The empowerment to be spiritually "free" to worship and create new songs that express the love and faith of bonded servants at work and worship continues. Prayers, sermons, and songs continually burst forth with symbols and metaphors that express the depths of faith, hope, and love embedded in the soul of the community and individuals. Whether offered spontaneously or with careful preparation, the metaphors provide perceptions about the realities of life while envisioning and celebrating the future. Worship can be viewed as both praise and empowerment, as it enables communities of faith to claim the "right to the tree of life" and act as agents of love and justice in the world.

Empowerment means experiencing and feeling freedom as "realized eschatology" in, but not limited to, corporate worship. African American worshipers have built upon the model of slave foreparents who became an eschatological community, praising the risen Lord in their midst as if this *kairotic* moment were the end of time. To "have church" is to experience Christ in the breaking of the bread at Communion, in baptism, in the breaking open of the bread of life in the preached and sung Word, and in the love flow of the gathered community. Where two, three, or more are gathered in Christ's name, divine intervention occurs.[3] Change, or *metanoia*, and a new identity are anticipated. Burdens, work loads, and imposed negative labels no longer matter. In these eschatological moments, a glimmer of hope is seen in the midst of struggle and suffering.

On this point, the historical merger of psychology and ecclesiology is quite helpful. Slave narratives are replete with references to slaveholders who tried to pour doctrinal beliefs into the heads and onto the lips of bonded servants who had no input into their shaping. The fixed doctrinal statements and rigidly defined systems of beliefs taught by missionaries were meaningless until the new convert could experience a relationship with the Divine through what was felt rather than what one was told to believe. To truly know and believe in God the Father, Jesus the Son, and the empowering Holy Spirit necessitates an encounter. Untutored slave poets could describe the love and compassion of Jesus in song because they had walked and talked with him as they worked and worshiped. Continuing in this tradition, the psychological release one experiences while passionately feeling the divine presence and singing about it far surpasses cerebral recitations that were (appropriately) shaped by a community of faith in a totally different context.

African Americans, empowered with freedom to praise God and eat at the Lord's "welcome table," receive further empowerment where love, shared common threads of culture, and circumstances are real. As the community of faith receives and experiences validation, there is no need to ponder the question, Why are we subjected to such an oppressed and marginalized status? Instead, a new social order is constructed, legitimated, and maintained in the light of their own hearing of the good news in Jesus the Christ. A religion of survival that facilitates divine power for actions of justice, epitomized in worship, actually empowers worshipers to hear God speak directly to them. From this hearing, worshipers are able to respond in ways that shape and reshape the liturgy so that love, hope, and solidarity can remain alive. Struggle for empowerment continues, for the danger of disempowerment looms ominous. In addition to societal injustices, which are in constant conflict with biblical teachings, there is the matter of verbal and nonverbal language that can degrade and disempower persons because of race, color, creed, gender, age, and physical impairment. Body language can communicate thoughts that speak louder than words. A person's sense of empowerment is affected by nonverbal thoughts expressed in negative actions toward her or him. The use of words, a cultural tool that serves as a means of human communication, reveals the power of verbal language to shape and define persons and symbols, create images, and interpret biblical truths. Words also have the power to shape attitudes and personal identity and can subconsciously affect personhood, interpersonal relationships, and the potential empowerment of humans. Words can limit or broaden one's understanding of God. To allow for expanded images and perceptions of God will positively affect and influence a community's perception of itself. The language of the liturgy, which spills over into life, should lend itself to helping individuals and communities realize their maximum potential.

Psychological Empowerment

Although a number of disciplines converge in the study of Christian worship, the psychological dimension is vital in an understanding of worship as empowerment. Various aspects of a person's total being are among the basic needs to be satisfied in an encounter with the Wholly Other. One of the most often celebrated dimensions of African Americans is the involvement of the whole person in worship. Holistic worship can lead to physical and psychological healing and wholeness.

The gift of faith involves a conscious understanding of God incarnate in Jesus in historical and current realities. In addition to physical and safety needs, there are modes of conscious activities and attitudes—feeling, knowing, and willing—which function together, often simultaneously and interdependently, in worship. These modes are affected by circumstances of life (existential situations) as well as by symbols and acts of worship. Knowing involves recognizing the object of worship and those with whom one worships. Feeling involves certain emotions, such as trust, love, fear, and anger, as well as perceptions. Willing involves choices, decisions, and commitments, which are expressed in outward (physical) activities such as service in mission and ministry.

In order for corporate worship to be authentic and empowering, it must be psychologically relevant to worshipers and commensurate with their lived experiences. One entering and reentering God's divine drama in worship should be enabled to maintain a connecting link to "God's unfolding story."[4] If worshipers can identify with the story through familiar symbols, actions, and familial relationships, their sense of belongingness will be enhanced, and empowerment is likely to take place. Sane survival in a perceptibly insane living environment is facilitated through the shaping and enacting of God's story in ritual action that offers praise to God and allows physical and mental catharsis. The important therapeutic role of worship in African American pastoral care is underscored by Edward Wimberly. Utilizing the concept that worship is "an act of people in a local church as they . . . celebrate and give praise to God for being drawn into God's story," Wimberly contends that worship is also a celebration of the fact that worshipers "have found meaning and purpose in their lives."[5] The depth of God's story includes God's defeat of the powers of evil, oppression, and suffering, as well as a story of healing and wholeness when people lead meaningful lives.[6] From their slave journey into the present time, African Americans celebrate these facts in ways that meet the psychological needs of the community and empower them to action. Like their ancient African ancestors, African Americans acquire coping skills without the aid of professional psychiatrists.

The importance of the therapeutic nature of emotional expression in African American worship is the concern of many scholars. Emotional forms of worship are also viewed as a way of producing and advancing an escapist mentality. At the height of religious fervor, one may escape or transcend personal problems and anxieties. Slave narratives provide extant records of the purging and cathartic effect of the ecstatic dimensions of worship. It is, therefore, not possible to deny the catharsis effected by emotionally induced worship. Any release of tension resulting from repressed emotions is better than some of the alternatives available. One's deliberate seeking for an encounter with the Almighty in worship may also result in a mystical encounter with the Divine that affords psychological release.

The mystic theologian Howard Thurman is helpful in his reminder that the total person is involved in authentic experiences. However, the person is obligated to move forward from the experience into a new life. Included in the totality of the person is a preliminary understanding of the meaning of the term *God* (or "preliminary residue of God meaning"), previous experiences, context of meanings, and values by which the *persona* is defined. One who approaches God "smelling of life," according to Thurman, is able to consciously realize what is happening. God meets individuals not only at personal levels of need, but also at the level of "residue of God meaning."[7]

Since worshipers come just as they are, there is the reality that some may come seeking to hide from themselves. Worship may provide an escape mechanism for unresolved psychological problems. Experiences of personal pain may be so deeply buried in the subconscious that one may appear to function well at a surface level, both in one's demeanor and in one's responses to others. Outward demonstrations may be ever so jubilant, when inside the psychological problems are like time bombs, waiting to explode. What appears on the surface as empowerment could be in actuality a releasing of tension in preparation for empowerment. In reference to such situations, William Willimon contends that tools of psychology can help one transcend the situation that provides a perspective from which meaning begins to arise out of what remains.[8]

Through ritual structure and anti-structure, African Americans are enabled to see, feel, and know God objectively—truly transcendent. Responses in worship acknowledge that God "is," and does not depend on humans for existence. The objective dimension, which is the starting point of worship, affirms emphatically that there is a God who loves and intervenes in the lives of humans.

Through rituals and symbols, worshipers are enabled to participate subjectively in worship as they envision themselves as vital and necessary actors in God's story. The subjective-objective dialogical interaction, often depicted in a latinized form of the cross, is necessarily held in tension in holistic worship. Worshipers come just as they are to respond as individuals and as members of the community of faith. Their *leitourgia* involves reaching upward to feel the presence and power of God and yielding to this power; reaching inward to feel and "hear" the internal heartbeat, the voice of the soul; and reaching outward to feel through touch those already reaching as well as those who have not yet learned how to reach.

Motivations that determine the current work of the people (liturgy) of particular communities and the extent to which certain practices are psychologically effective are varied and not always transferable. In some instances, African Americans at worship carry on certain ritual practices without question simply because "they have always done it a certain way." Some will refer to particular elements or practices as the way Black folk "ought" to worship, as if there is an African American orthodoxy ("right praise"). This reference disregards the uniqueness of local context, psychological dimensions, and the nontransferability of some of the worship practices.

No one predetermined set of ritual actions can be packaged to meet the needs of *all* worshiping African American communities. For an onlooker to discredit certain actions by relegating them to "non-Black" is not fair to the communities who have struggled to determine the right praise for those who gather together regularly. Perhaps what is being encouraged by those who assume that there is an African American orthodoxy is that the community not lose touch with its history. To have "come this far by faith" is to recognize that God continually intervenes and guides the faith walk. There are unique worship actions that were shaped out of common, fundamental, primal world views, symbols, and metaphors. Coping skills are still necessary in a postmodern society. Nevertheless, every age dictates a reevaluation of contexts, needs, and missional thrusts so that ritual action does not become "empty praise."

Ministry and Mission

As indicated throughout the history of African American worship, the need for sacred space both evolved from and enhanced the opportunity for ministry. Corporate worship was and remains the foundation and context for the ministry of mutual pastoral care and nurture in the faith. Initially, the immediate corporate missional task was to seek ways to survive and to attain justice and freedom, which the Word of God had declared was rightfully theirs. This mission was often realized and actualized following worship in political revolutions and insurrections.[9] While these might not represent traditional understandings of missional acts or service, they represent for an oppressed people empowered engagement in the struggle for liberation. A very important mission for a people who claim a mutual "pilgrim's journey" in God's story is to render service by engaging in efforts to reconstruct an unjust society.

This missional thrust, which ultimately gained legal freedom for slaves and expanded the vision of oppressors, did not end with slavery. The "revolutionary" character of worship in action is basic to the life of Jesus. Inherent in the gospel message is a radical disapproval of the claim of power invested in a few who work vigorously to maintain the status quo. A part of the continual mission of congregations is to keep this biblical fact before all who, through baptism and in the Lord's Supper, acknowledge their oneness in the body of Christ.

Paul is quite clear in his reminder in Romans 12 that worship extends beyond the bounds of the assembly into acts of service in the world. He was aware that the celebration of the Lord's Supper, when it is overly sacramentalized, could lead to abuses in worship. This could be overcome only by a change in ethical relationships in the community (1 Cor. 11:17ff.). Current practices often overlook the teachings of Jesus as recorded in Matthew 5:23-24, which calls for worshipers to be reconciled with brothers and sisters before offering a gift. The implication here is that there is more to worship than merely performing rituals. Walls separating the sacred and the secular, which were torn down by Jesus, are raised by human hands when worshipers separate the ritual waters of baptism from the table fellowship acts of service in the world. A reconnecting of sacred and secular undergirds the mission of the peaceful revolution led by Martin Luther King, Jr., and continues in many organized efforts led by African Americans. In true and authentic worship of God there is a dialectical relationship rather than a dichotomy between faith and practice, justice and ritual action (liturgy and justice), theological talk and doxological living, and sanctification and human liberation.

One must also understand that early mission and ministry in the Black community included service to God through evangelical efforts within the community. Evangelization was not limited to Euro-American missional efforts. African Americans were at the forefront of faith sharing as they reached out to bring others into the fold.

Corporate worship continues today in the *diakonia* as the church scatters in the mission of Jesus the Christ in service to the world. A worshiping community in mission is evidence of God's empowering and sending the church forth to verbally spread the good news and to live the faith so that the love of God can be seen and heard in the actions of persons and communities. The needs and concerns of the poor, the hungry, the homeless, those affected by wars, and those still in bondage anywhere in the world are to be attended. As long as people continue to live in these circumstances, radical liberation is needed.

Empowerment enables individuals, local congregations, and interdenominational and civic groups committed to the work of Christ to exercise compassion in works of reconciliation, justice, and peace.'

Sharing of African American Liturgical Traditions

The New Testament understanding of liturgy, which has suffered loss in translation, is that Christ's life, death, and resurrection are, in fact, the epitome of liturgy. Christians who claim that their lives are in Christ are formed and shaped by the likeness of Christ, and are an embodiment of efforts to make present this *one* liturgy in all times and places. This is to say that Jesus' life of worship as God incarnate, both in ritual actions and in ethical responses to the holy, is the ultimate model of worship. We truly worship as we are empowered by the Holy Spirit to embody Christ present in and through us.

The most effective demonstration of true liturgy is what we do in obedience to God in Christ with our lives when we gather and when we scatter as a community in the world. To participate obediently drives worshipers to earnestly desire both the assembly and the scattering. Life in the world always calls one back to mutual companionship in gatherings, confession of sin, pardon, and renewal. Empowered gatherings evoke the need to go forth into the world to love and serve in spite of the fact that the world and the worshiper are unfortunately not always compassionate and loving.

As the Holy Spirit works through the people's work, transformation of time, worshipers, and the world is made possible. No participation in ritual action, whether culturally understood or borrowed from other cultures, can be renewing if the intent of the Christ event is not rooted in a true desire of the worshiper to be transformed. If one approaches the holy meal with blinders so that those gathered at other tables are not also seen through the "mind's eye," regardless of differences, one cannot truly see Christ in one's neighbor.

If worshipers are deliberate in their attempt to incorporate ritual actions of others, they must be clear about *why* they want to do so. Ritual action cannot be injected (as with a hypodermic needle) into a community's liturgy or liturgical life. The corporate nature of the assembly is a decisive factor in the enhancement of liturgy. This must be clear as the starting point for an effective grounding of actions. Corporate worship is indeed an important starting place for worshipers to appropriate faith traditions so that the lived experiences of others might be understood. African Americans have adapted and assimilated liturgical actions from other cultures by redefining the actions in the light of their own lived experiences. For some worshipers, the elimination of prejudices against certain cultures and people must begin with reeducation and reconciliation before learning can take place. A divinely empowered encounter with God at a deeper level, basic to worship, can take place as worshipers experience ritual action that evolved through another's faith experience.

With an understanding of the theological undergirding and importance of a holistic approach to planning for the worship experience, suggestions for incorporating elements of singing, preaching, praying, and a hospitable community environment will follow. The suggestions offered here are applicable in *any* situation to the extent that they provide spiritual renewal for the worshipers.

Singing

The current trend of including Spirituals, hymns, and Gospel songs in predominantly Euro-American denominational hymnals is important for liturgical enrichment.[10] Equally significant are trends of development and revision of hymnals by African American denominations. In addition to standard Euro-American hymns, many hymnals include a broader repertoire of African American music. What is communicated in recent hymnal publications is an acknowledgment of the liturgical appropriation of

African American faith experiences. Also helpful is an acknowledgment of specific racial ethnic sources of texts and tunes. Prior to this trend, compilers simply employed such terms as "American folk song," "traditional," and "anonymous" to identify music of racial ethnic origins. The use of inclusive language in hymnody is not yet an area of concern in many African American congregations.

Many songs from African American traditions are appropriate in worship for a variety of uses throughout the church year. With careful planning and with the aid of hymnal indexes, songs from other traditions can become an integral and viable part of worship. Poetic expressions from the souls and struggles of any people can broaden one's understanding of God's divine empowerment in all ages.[11]

Although congregations are generally more comfortable with certain styles, forms, tempos, and musical accompaniments, there is no reason they should be limited to only music that pleases them. Music leaders should seek information about history, form, diversity of music styles and tempos before introducing music from a culture other than their own. By so doing, they will discover that there are manners of presentation that will facilitate the use of new and different music. Equipped with history and tradition, an alert musician will seek to blend the experiences of the congregation with the originators of the music being introduced. Leaders should avoid applying a "normative performance standard" set by a culture other than the one in which the music originated.

There is tremendous value in ecumenical and cross-cultural worship, workshops, and festivals where music traditions can be shared. Theological schools, where pastors, musicians, and Christian educators are preparing for ministry, are also good environments where this kind of sharing can take place. At least one school, the Interdenominational Theological Center in Atlanta, Georgia, is intentional in its effort to maintain and enhance African American Christian worship and music styles, while also facilitating the student's exposure to and appreciation for ecumenical forms and styles.

African American song forms are rooted in Spirituals, a religious folk song genre that lends itself to a continuous shaping process. This means, then, that relegation to a "campfire usage" mentality goes counter to its intent. Black Gospel songs were born in the church and are most effective as a worship form without a "stage performance" orientation. Both genres are mediums through which praise can be offered to God, and God's empowering Word can be heard and felt. Both genres are also

115

diverse in form and style, ranging from slow and plaintive to fast and highly syncopated. When *any* music in worship becomes performance only and a form of entertainment, it ceases to be praise offered to God.

Preaching

Current writings by African Americans on Black preaching are sufficiently numerous so that any preacher sincerely interested in learning from the preaching traditions can be informed.[12] There are also numerous books of sermons by Black preachers, including women preachers, which provide diverse models of styles and intentionality.[13] The cautions raised previously about superficial "injections" of liturgical elements merely for the sake of being inclusive also prevail in sharing this element of worship.

Among the salient factors are the centrality of preaching in worship, the care exercised by Black preachers in the hermeneutical process, and the necessary relevance in the preaching style and content, so that the Word is understood by the congregation. An important characteristic of hermeneutics in Black preaching is the empowerment of the preacher to create an atmosphere wherein the preacher and listener might hear the Word by experiencing it. The preacher must be so familiar with the story that he or she, during the preaching moment, becomes the biblical character, the carrier of the letter from the epistle writer to the people, the paralytic who needs healing, or the woman with the issue of blood. The *sitz im leben* ("situation in life") of the text is internalized so that it is transformed, and it comes alive to the context of the preacher. The goal is to create an atmosphere in which the listeners can themselves become the Word of God incarnate at the moment. The artistic dimensions of this process are described by Henry Mitchell as follows: "The goal of Black preaching is to recreate a meaningful experience which communicates transconsciously, nourishing the whole human being. This is indeed high art."[14]

The atmosphere is intellectual, experiential, and emotional as the storyteller gives an eyewitness account that facilitates the congregation's visualizing, claiming ownership, and relating to the text. This form of storytelling combines the art of living the experience and freedom for the empowering of the Holy Spirit. By so doing the congregation can participate in the story as it is empowered to do so. Just how the participatory response happens (or takes place) is not dependent solely upon the fact that the congregation is African American. Again, there is no one response that emerges by virtue of race. The context, the occasion, the message, and the preacher's style may evoke a multitude of responses. Interactional dialogue between the preacher and the pew is determined by the movement of the Spirit, the context, and the form of genuine response that the congregation is generally most comfortable with. There may be simple body language such as the nodding of the head in assent, a smile, tears, or more demonstrable responses such as the throwing or waving of a handkerchief toward the preacher, standing, or shouting as the story strikes a familiar chord in the life of the worshiper.

One feature of the preaching moment emphasized by Henry Mitchell is the sermon celebration as relevant empowerment. He proposes in his methodology for teaching preaching that "instead of simply winding down and taking a seat, the preacher-performing artist engages in a final, triumphant or celebrative expression of the theme or the resolution of conflict or issue."[15]

This form of celebration is not exhortation nor is it a manipulative way to create an emotional "charge." It is a celebrative affirmation and a form of challenge for people to enact or demonstrate what they claim to celebrate. As should be apparent, these concepts cannot be imported in toto, even if one is clear about the spiritual intentionality or effectiveness.

The recovery of preaching as story or storytelling has recently emerged among Euro-Americans as a form that lends itself to a renewal of preaching.[16] Perhaps a review of the historical style of Black preaching, which is rooted in the African *griot* and continues without interruption into the present century, would enhance the effectiveness of this style of preaching. Sincerity in preparing and delivering the Word of God and openness to the empowerment of the Holy Spirit must prevail!

Prayer

The unique forms and styles of prayer in African American worship, like other unique elements of worship, are rooted and grounded in African traditional religions. In both settings, people of African descent highlight thanksgiving for God's immanent presence in nature and all of life. There is the freedom to call upon God, who provides health, strength, and joy. Prayers spontaneously burst forth in joy for the opportunity "just to have a little talk with Jesus, who lies with me on my sick bed and keeps the blood running warm in my veins." The element of thanksgiving bursts forth despite the hard life to which the oppressed are subjected.

The words of traditional prayers, like the prayers of the saints and martyrs of Euro-America, could enhance and broaden an awareness of other people of the faith. Elements of spontaneity are already included in current worshiping practices. These could be expanded so that simple elements of life are acknowledged. The authors of *Prayer in World Religions* have observed that penitential aspects of ritual and prayer under the impact of a pessimistic view of human nature have been stressed during many periods of history. They are helpful in their suggestion that

> African [and in this instance, African American] prayer suggests a healthy corrective of this potentially dolorous Christian spirituality. If people were to thank God for the light of their eyes and the air they breathed . . . and the light of their minds, they would be less inclined to fall into the preoccupation with self that has mottled Christian prayer.[17]

Constraint in the use of the prayers of others is understandable, because prayer in all communities is so personal and basic to the soul of the community. This could explain why many African Americans tend to avoid using prayers from other traditions. Nevertheless, care should be taken that prayer in worship does not become an individual prayer prayed in public.

Shared learning can take place as the realities of all of life permeate worship. This fact comes to life as one dares to look around to watch the facial expressions of others during prayer time. As the pray-er calls upon God for intercession in situations in the world or in the lives of those assembled, worshipers are prone to "voice" a silent or verbal "amen" with confidence that God will answer the prayer. Prayer should reflect hope in the midst of the experiences of a community.

Community

When God calls the community to assemble for worship, all humanly contrived social distinctions and "isms" are to be transcended. All are equal in the sight of God, and all are equally loved by God. Therefore, the experience of a beloved community is central to worship. The extent to which community togetherness happens depends on whether worshipers intentionally seek to transcend those things that divide us. There is no true corporate worship if there is no togetherness. An instrumental prelude may be able to focus attention on the music being produced, but it cannot, in and of itself, create a beloved community.

An important gift from the African American community is its focus on the time of gathering as a time of hospitality, a time of reentry into God's space, a time of spiritual heightening and "leveling." When the flow of the service is an appropriate blend of freedom within form, spontaneity within order, this time for unifying the community might be extended. Under the power of the Holy Spirit, worshipers are guided through periods of praise, thanksgiving, personal testimonies, and prayers, which engage the entire congregation.

It is suggested that worshiping communities reevaluate the intent of the period of preparation or prelude, which is a vital aspect of the liturgical flow. If worshipers are inclined to assume an attitude of "business as usual" at the earliest part of the service, the process of change should be gradual rather than disruptive. This will require teaching, lots of discussion, sensitivity, and openness to trust the power of the Spirit among the worship leaders, especially musicians. A time of gathering could alternate between traditional modes and whatever form of bonding the community will attempt.

The community's freedom—uninhibited freedom—to respond to God's Word and the Holy Spirit's empowerment is an aspect of African American worship that facilitates all acts of worship. One cannot superimpose uninhibited freedom in worship on an assembly that has been "taught" to be passive by simply following the printed order of service. Careful planning and sensitive leadership can help in the freeing process. There is no one method, no one prescribed formula for this process. Openness and sensitivity to the total environment on the part of leadership are absolutely necessary!

One danger in all of this is that congregations might find themselves "enjoying the Lord" so much that they assume that this is to happen only when one gathers to worship informally. Another danger is that congregations might assume that all services of worship must be jubilant in order for authentic worship to take place. There is always the possibility that Christ has entered the sacred space with a whip to drive out the thieves and money changers—those who have allowed ritual actions to become empty. Empowered worship is a divine act engendered and facilitated by the One who wrote and holds the libretto—God incarnate in Jesus the Christ!

Worship Planning in African American Churches

All persons responsible for the planning of worship should recognize that a sufficient amount of time is necessary for careful preparation. Although there might be denominational differences as to persons responsible for worship, there is great value in team efforts in the planning process. This might include the pastor(s), and a worship committee (or commission) involving leaders of worship, such as musicians, liturgists (called presiding officers or worship leaders in some churches), and lay members—adults, youth, and children of the congregation. Worship planned far enough in advance will allow musicians an opportunity to explore musical options and select and prepare music in keeping with the flow of the service, according to Scriptures and themes of the day. Although familiar congregational music facilitates participation, new songs and alternative language can be introduced when worship leaders coordinate efforts.

Team work, under the power of the Spirit, also allows the shaping of prayers, sermons, and other liturgical elements to be interwoven into a harmonious whole without impeding spontaneity. Meaningful, creative planning will free congregations to reclaim and utilize historical elements of the tradition, and allow an incorporation of artistic gifts and resources available in the congregation and local community. Planning unleashes the ability of worship leaders to listen for directions in making smooth transitions in the flow of the service. This is one of the many gifts of Black church worship that should be recovered or continued. Planning will also allow leaders to hear from the community that worship elements and actions have become "empty rituals" and help determine where education in workshops might be necessary.

The following suggestions are offered:

1. *Consider the lived experiences of worshipers and their understanding of worship.*
2. *Consider the worship space.* What images, symbols, and moods are conveyed? Are African American symbols present? What is the central focus? What theological understandings does the worship space reflect? Are these understandings consistent with your denominational theology? Is the space aesthetically appealing? Are there seasonal banners? Where are the sources of

120

light? Does the space draw your body and being into a realm of imaginative reverence? Is the space cluttered? Is it bare? Is there wasted space? Can the space be rearranged without destroying a feeling of worshipfulness? Is the chancel space divided? Is the choir located so that it facilitates its leadership in worship? Do plush carpet and seat cushions interfere with the acoustics so that microphones are necessary?

3. *Become familiar with your denominational polity and theology of worship to determine what elements are required and what your denomination believes about each of the elements.* Attention should also be given to restrictions and options. How often is the Lord's Supper to be celebrated? Where are the Lord's Supper and baptism placed in the order of service? Why? Be intentional about examining theological implications when "borrowing" from denominational traditions other than your own.

4. *Use Scripture to undergird the entire worship event.* The use of a lectionary would be helpful, but is not required. Each of the elements in the order of worship should reflect an interweaving of the Scripture(s) and the sermon, so that the congregation might be led to a well-rounded worship experience.

5. *Consider the flow of the service to determine what pattern facilitates worship in the particular congregation.* For instance, is the service simply an alternation between spoken words and singing, standing and sitting, listening and responding? Are acts of worship empty ritual—merely perfunctory and highly predictable? Does the service flow around a particular theme of the day, or does it simply follow the format of a "variety program" for which the pastor liturgist serves as announcer?

6. *Take care that the language of the liturgy is inclusive.* This means verbal and printed language (Scriptures, songs, sermon, prayers, announcements) as well as nonverbal language, including well-represented leadership! Much is communicated through the involvement of persons and the ways that they are involved.

Although denominations may vary as to the content and exact order of service, the following model is generally reflective of worship planning in African American congregations. The location of the Lord's Supper and baptism have been excluded, because they will depend on denominational theology and polity.

WORSHIP MODEL

A TIME OF GATHERING

As people gather, they may greet one another, extend hospitality, and then prepare for worship with quiet meditation. This may also be a period of devotions with informal prayers, reading of Scripture, singing, and testimonies. Related activities might include announcements (community concerns) or rehearsal of new congregational music. An instrumental or choral prelude appropriate to the season of the church year may signal the end of this period. Acolytes may light the candles.

CALL TO WORSHIP

Scriptural sentences or words that proclaim that God in Jesus the Christ has taken the initiative to call the people to worship. This may be sung by the choir or choir and congregation, spoken by a leader, or read responsively.

OPENING PRAYER

This prayer (prayer of the day, Collect, or Invocation) should include elements of adoration and praise to God, who in Jesus the Christ continues to make worship opportunities possible. The leader should be reminded that the Holy Spirit is not to be manipulated!

OPENING HYMN OR SONG OF PRAISE AND ADORATION

(Could be a processional.) The focus of this hymn or song should continue the praise to God and should *not* focus on human needs or conditions.

PRAYER OF CONFESSION

The community of faith should acknowledge its propensity to sin. This prayer may be offered by the leader on behalf of the congregation or prayed in unison by the leader and congregation. A period of silent confession may precede or follow the prayer and a Kyrie ("Lord, have mercy") may be sung.

STATEMENT OF ASSURANCE OF PARDON

God's forgiving love and mercy are declared for all who with sincerity repent of their sins.

GLORIA PATRI/DOXOLOGY/SONG OF THANKSGIVING

A trinitarian ascription of praise or a song of thanksgiving may be sung by the congregation as a reminder that God's promise of forgiveness is a gift of grace, for which we are ever grateful.

***WELCOME OF VISITORS

The gathered community is welcomed, with special attention to visitors, who are encouraged early in the service to participate fully as a part of the extended family. This provides an additional opportunity for hospitality to be extended.

COMMUNITY CONCERNS AND ANNOUNCEMENTS

These elements occurring together allow for intentional involvement of the laity. If announcements are printed in the bulletin, these need not be read aloud unless local congregational needs so dictate or certain concerns need to be highlighted. This element could lead to the pastoral prayer or prayers of thanksgiving and intercession.

(PASTORAL PRAYER/PRAYERS OF INTERCESSION/ OR ALTAR CALL)

In some traditions, a prayer at this point might include an "altar call," which allows an opportunity for individuals to come forward for special prayer needs as a way of laying their burdens on the altar of God. A hymn of personal surrendering might be sung prior to the prayer.

ANTHEM/SPIRITUAL/GOSPEL SONG

In African American congregations where there are choirs or a single choir, the offering of praise in song might be an extension of praise on behalf of the people gathered. The use of children's choirs as an essential part of worship is highly encouraged.

(OFFERTORY)

The placement of the offertory at this point has a more practical than theological rationale. There are also several opportunities for offering, and this placement might be for benevolent or mission offering. The focus on total stewardship as a call from God might eliminate the plethora of offerings in worship. A musical offering could also be made at this time (choir, soloist, instrumentalist).

THE SPOKEN WORD OF GOD

SCRIPTURE(S)

It is appropriate for passages from both the Old and the New Testaments to be read. Care should be taken to allow the choice of Scripture(s) to be foundational to other elements.

CONGREGATIONAL SONG

The music offered here should relate to the sermon. In some settings the song might be eliminated, so that the preacher moves directly from Scripture to the sermon.

SERMON

One or more of the Scripture readings would provide the text for the sermon. Faithful preaching confronts the people with the liberating, renewing Word of God, and witnesses to God's continuing activity among the people in and through Jesus the Christ. The preacher should serve as a conduit through which God speaks.

RESPONSE TO THE WORD OF GOD

INVITATION TO DISCIPLESHIP (ALTAR CALL)

The call to discipleship is a continuation of God's call for the people to live the worship that they experience, to renew their commitment to discipleship, or to come forward for special prayer needs. This element may also symbolize an "opening of the doors" of the church in order to receive new members.

SONG OR HYMN OF AFFIRMATION OR COMMITMENT

This song is appropriately sung as a part of the invitation to discipleship (and altar call), and should reflect the message of the sermon. It can be more personally oriented, because it is a reminder of one's commitment to discipleship.

***OFFERTORY

The offertory placed at this point in the service follows the theological understanding that one's giving of oneself to God includes all that one is and possesses. The symbolic offering (full surrendering) of oneself should be the focus and not merely "the giving" of monetary gifts.

SENDING AND GOING FORTH

SONG OR HYMN

In anticipation of the benediction, the focus of this song is the unity of the worshipers as they prepare to scatter to serve in the world. This may be a recessional song for the choir, to symbolize the sending and going forth of the community. In keeping with the Scripture, the people have been nurtured by the Word, and now they sing a hymn as they prepare to leave.

CHARGE AND BENEDICTION

The pastor faces the people and charges them to go forth, using words that capture the essence of the message. A blessing is then given, with the pastor looking into the faces of the people as they are blessed.

POSTLUDE

Worshipers may remain seated in silent meditation, or they may leave. Care should be taken to encourage those who choose to leave not to unduly disturb those who are seated in silent meditation.

***Where this symbol appears, worship planners may include additional music, creeds, or other appropriate acts of worship. Parenthetical elements indicate optional locations of these acts of worship.

For Discussion

1. Is there a difference between "empowerment to be" and "empowerment to do"? Explain your answer.

2. What in your experience has been the most empowering dimension of worship? Is it always or sometimes the entire worship service or particular elements of worship?

3. Team planning can be difficult. How would you organize planning sessions to facilitate the coordination of elements of worship?

4. Work with a team to plan a service of worship that will incorporate elements in keeping with your denominational suggestions and requirements.

Rules for the Society of Negroes. 1693.

We the Miserable Children of *Adam*, and of *Noah*, thankfully Admiring and Accepting the Free-Grace of GOD, that Offers to Save us from our Miseries, by the Lord Jesus Christ, freely Resolve, with His Help, to become the Servants of that Glorious LORD.

And that we may be Assisted in the Service of our *Heavenly Master,* we now Join together in a SOCIETY, wherein the following RULES are to be observed.

I. It shall be our Endeavour, to Meet in the Evening after the Sabbath; and Pray together by Turns, one to Begin, and another to Conclude the Meeting; And between the two *Prayers,* a *Psalm* shall be Sung, and a *Sermon* Repeated.

II. Our coming to the Meeting, shall never be without the *Leave* of such as have power over us: And we will be Careful, that our Meeting may Begin and Conclude between the Hours of *Seven* and *Nine*; and that we may not be *unseasonably* Absent from the Families whereto we pertain.

III. As we will, with the Help of God, at all Times avoid all *Wicked Company,* so we will Receive none into our Meeting, but such as have sensibly *Reformed* their Lives from all manner of Wickedness. And therefore, None shall be Admitted, without the Knowledge and Consent of the Minister of God in this Place; unto whom we will also carry every Person, that seeks for *Admission* among us; to be by Him Examined, Instructed and Exhorted.

Reprinted from Thomas J. Holmes, *Cotton Mather: A Bibliography of His Works* (Cambridge, Mass., 1940).

IV. We will, as often as may be, Obtain some Wife and Good Man, of the *English* in the Neighbourhood, and especially the Officers of the Church, to look in upon us, and by their Presence and Council, do what they think fitting for us.

V. If any of our Number, fall into the Sin of *Drunkenness*, or *Swearing*, or *Cursing*, or *Lying*, or *Stealing*, or notorious *Disobedience* or *Unfaithfulness* into their Masters, we will *Admonish* him of his Miscarriage, and Forbid his coming to the Meeting, for at least *one Fortnight*; And except he then come with great Signs and Hopes of his *Repentance*, we will utterly Exclude him, with Blotting his *Name* out of our List.

VI. If any of our Society Defile himself with Fornication, we will give him our *Admonition*; and so, debar him from the Meeting, at least *half a Year*: Nor shall he Return to it, ever any more, without Exemplary Testimonies of his becoming a *New Creature*.

VII. We will, as we have Opportunity, set our selves to do all the Good we can, to the other *Negro-Servants* in the Town; And if any of them should, at unfit Hours, be *Abroad*, much more, if any of them should *Run away* from their Masters, we will afford them *no Shelter*: But we will do what in us lies, that they may be discovered, and punished. And if any *of us*, are found Faulty, in this Matter, they shall be no longer *of me*.

VIII. None of our Society shall be *Absent* from our Meeting, without giving a *Reason* of the Absence; And if it be found, that any have pretended unto their *Owners*, that they came unto the *Meeting*, when they were otherwise and elsewhere Employ'ed, we will faithfully *Inform* their Owners, and also do what we can to Reclaim such Person from all such Evil Courses for the Future.

IX. It shall be expected from every one in the Society, that he learn the *Catechism*: And therefore, it shall be one of our usual Exercises, for one of us, to ask the *Questions*, and for all the rest in their Order to say the *Answers* in the *Catechism*; Either, The *New-English* Catechism, or the *Assemblies* Catechism, or the Catechism in the *Negro Christianized*.

NOTES

1. A Theology of African American Worship

1. See John S. Mbiti, *Concepts of God in Africa* (New York: Praeger, 1970), chaps. 8–13.
2. See Mechal Sobel, *Trabelin' On* (Princeton, N.J.: Princeton University Press, 1979), pp. 3–21. See also Thomas Luckman, *The Invisible Religion: The Problem of Religion in Modern Society* (New York: Macmillan, 1967), pp. 52–54; Peter L. Berger, *The Sacred Canopy* (Garden City, N.Y.: Anchor Books, 1969); Peter L. Berger and Thomas Luckman, *The Social Construction of Reality* (London: Penguin Book Press, 1966).
3. For an African American Episcopalian perspective, see *Lift Every Voice and Sing II: An African American Hymnal* (New York: The Church Hymnal Corporation, 1993), especially the preface. For an African American United Methodist perspective, see William B. McClain, *Come Sunday: The Liturgy of Zion* (Nashville: Abingdon Press, 1990), pp. 48–71. For an African American Catholic perspective, see Mary E. McGann, *A Precious Fountain: Music and Worship of an African American Catholic Community* (Collegeville, Minn.: Liturgical Press, 2004); J-Glenn Murray, "The Liturgy of the Roman Rite and African American Worship," in *Lead Me, Guide Me: The African American Catholic Hymnal* (Chicago: GIA Publications, 1987), pp. xi-xv; and Clarence Joseph Rivers, *The Spirit in Worship* (Cincinnati: Clarence Joseph Rivers, 1978), pp. 77–97. For an African American Lutheran perspective, see *This Far By Faith: An African American Resource for Worship* (Minneapolis: Augsburg Fortress, 1999). For an African American Presbyterian perspective, see Gayraud Wilmore, *Black and Presbyterian: The Heritage and the Hope*, rev. and enl. (Louisville: Witherspoon Press, 1998).
4. See James H. Cone, *Black Theology and Black Power* (New York: The Seabury Press, 1969). For a summary of the origin of Black Theology, see James H. Cone, *For My People: Black Theology and the Black Church* (Maryknoll, N.Y.: Orbis Books, 1984), pp. 5–30.
5. See Melva W. Costen and Darius L. Swann, eds., *The Black Christian Worship Experience*, rev. ed., Black Church Scholar Series, vol. IV (Atlanta: The ITC Press, 1992); Leonard E. Barrett, *Soul-Force: African Heritage in Afro-American Religion* (Garden City, N.Y.: Anchor Press/Doubleday, 1974); Nicholas C. Cooper-Lewter and Henry H. Mitchell, *Soul Theology* (San Franscisco: Harper & Row, 1986; paperback edition, Nashville: Abingdon Press, 1991); James H. Cone, *Speaking the Truth* (Grand Rapids: Eerdmans, 1986); Eugene D. Genovese, *Roll, Jordan, Roll* (New York: Vintage Books, 1974); Robert E. Hood, *Must God Remain Greek?* (Minneapolis: Fortress Press, 1990); Lawrence W. Levine, *Black Culture and Black Consciousness* (New York: Oxford University Press, 1977); C. Eric Lincoln and Lawrence H. Mamiya, *The Black Church in the African American Experience* (Durham, N.C.: Duke University Press, 1990); Gayraud S. Wilmore, *Black Religion and Black Radicalism*, 2nd ed. (Maryknoll, N.Y.: Orbis Books, 1983); Gayraud S. Wilmore, ed., *African American Religious Studies: An Interdisciplinary Anthology* (Durham, N.C.: Duke University Press, 1989).
6. See John S. Mbiti, *African Religions and Philosophy* (New York: Anchor/Doubleday, 1970), pp. 20–36. The concept of wholeness is deeply rooted in African understanding of being (ontology) in a world where everything is seen in relation to humans, the concept of time. Every mode of existence presupposes and depends on another. Unless there is unity in the cosmos, one cannot be totally whole.
7. See Peter L. Berger, *Facing Up to Modernity* (New York: Harper & Row, 1977); Douglas C. Bowman, *Beyond the Modern Mind* (New York: Pilgrim Press, 1990); Harvey Cox, *Religion in the Secular City: Toward a Postmodern Theology* (New York: Simon & Schuster, 1984).

8. See Mircea Eliade, *The Sacred & the Profane: The Nature of Religion* (New York: Harcourt Brace Jovanovich, 1959), pp. 116–25; Mbiti, *African Religions and Philosophy*, pp. 37–96.

9. See Melva Wilson Costen, "African Roots of Afro-American Baptismal Practices," in Costen and Swann, *The Black Christian Worship Experience*, pp. 23–42.

10. See Mbiti, *African Religions and Philosophy*, p. 75.

11. Cooper-Lewter and Mitchell, *Soul Theology*, p. 3. These authors contend that a new method and motivation for doing theology could begin with core belief or functional world views.

12. Sara Little contends that belief systems: (1) help persons find meaning and make sense of life; (2) help maintain community identity and continuity; (3) give Christian direction to life; and (4) link the individual and the community to ultimate reality and purpose. See Sara Little, *To Set One Heart* (Atlanta: John Knox Press, 1983), pp. 18–21.

13. Quoted in John S. Mbiti, *African Religions and Philosophy*, p. 38.

14. Ibid., p. 139.

15. Ibid., p. 136.

16. Ibid., p. 141.

17. Victor W. Turner, *The Ritual Process: Structure and Anti-Structure* (Ithaca, N.Y.: Cornell University Press, 1969).

18. Ibid., p. 129.

19. Mercy Amba Oduyoye, "The Value of African Religious Beliefs and Practices for Christian Theology," in *African Theology en Route*, ed. Kofi Appiah-Kubi and Sergio Torres (Maryknoll, N.Y.: Orbis Books, 1979), pp. 110–11.

2. The African Religious Heritage

1. See Benjamin Quarles, *The Negro in the Making of America*, rev. ed. (London: Collier-MacMillan, 1969), pp. 15–16.

2. See Lerone Bennett Jr., *Before the Mayflower: A History of Black America* (Chicago: Johnson Publishing Company, 1982), pp. 5–7. See also Cheikh Anta Diop, *The African Origin of Civilization*, trans. Mercer Cook (New York: Lawrence Hill & Company, 1974), pp. 260–75.

3. In addition to previous references to the rooting of Christianity in North Africa between A.D. 180 and 430, there is evidence that "colonial" Christianity was introduced to sub-Saharan Africa by way of the Portuguese. Persons of African descent were among the explorers in North and South America. They accompanied Pizarro in Peru, Cortes in Mexico, and Menendez in Florida. Thirty were with Balboa when he "discovered" the Pacific Ocean. Estevanico, perhaps the most famous of the early explorers of African origin, helped open New Mexico and Arizona for the Spaniards. Others accompanied DeSoto in his exploration missions, and one is reported to have stayed in Alabama, thus becoming among the first "foreign" settlers. See Bennett, *Before the Mayflower*, p. 34; Joseph Washington Jr., *Black Sects and Cults* (Garden City, N.Y.: Anchor Press/Doubleday, 1973), pp. 22–24.

4. See John Barbot, *A Description of the Coasts of North and South Guinea* (London: 1732), pp. 80, 104. See also John C. Messenger Jr., "Religious Acculturation Among the Anang Ibibio," in William R. Bascom and Melville J. Herskovits, eds., *Continuity and Change in African Cultures* (Chicago: University of Chicago Press, 1959), pp. 257–78.

5. See Ralph M. Wiltgen, *Gold Coast Mission History, 1471–1880* (Techny, Ill.: Divine Word Publication, 1956), pp. 11, 14–15. According to Wiltgen, Nzinga Mbemba was baptized on May 3, 1491. His son, Prince Henrique, was nominated bishop by Pope Leo X in 1518. For additional information about Nzinga Mbemba, Dom Affonso I, see also Basil Davidson, *The African Slave Trade* (Boston: Little, Brown & Company, 1961), pp. 117–62; and Georges Balandier, *Daily Life in the Kingdom of the Kongo* (New York: World Publishing Company, 1969), pp. 244–63.

6. See Eugene D. Genovese, *Roll, Jordan, Roll: The World the Slaves Made* (New York: Vintage Books, 1976), p. 176.

7. See Benjamin Brawley, *A Social History of the American Negro* (New York: MacMillan, 1921), p. 7. For a captivating post–Civil Rights view of this subject, see James T. Campbell, *Middle Passages: African American Journeys to Africa, 1787–2005* (New York: Penguin Press, 2006).
8. See Quarles, *The Negro in the Making of America*, p. 33. A slave converted to Christianity and baptized became enfranchised. This practice was based on the theory that, inasmuch as infidels were enslaved in order to make Christians of them, it followed that when the cause of their enslavement was removed, they would be granted freedom.
9. See Bennet, *Before the Mayflower*, pp. 37–41. Bennet provides accounts from public deeds of indentured servants who were freed. The now freed servants later bought servants, some of them white, and were granted land on the basis of the "headright" system, which permitted free land based on the number of servants acquired.
10. Ibid., p. 39.
11. Ibid., p. 44.
12. Cited in Edward D. Smith, *Climbing Jacob's Ladder: The Rise of Black Churches in Eastern American Cities, 1740–1877* (Washington, D.C.: Smithsonian Institution, for the Anacostia Museum, 1988), p. 27; see also Appendix, "Rules for the Society of Negroes, 1693."
13. See Appendix, "Rules for the Society of Negroes, 1693," rules II and IX.
14. In addition to Virginia and New England, settlements began in regions that would ultimately become Maryland (1634), North Carolina (1653), South Carolina (ca. 1670), and Georgia (1733). The latter colony initially forbade slavery but changed the law in 1749 to become a slave state. An excellent study of the relationship between slavery and Christianity during this period is provided by Lester B. Scherer, *Slavery and the Churches in Early America* (Grand Rapids: Eerdmans, 1975).
15. See Quarles, *The Negro in the Making of America*, p. 83.
16. See ibid., pp. 83–106. This chapter on the "Nonslave Negro (1800–1860)" helps provide a broader context for discussions on communal worship.
17. Vincent Harding, *There Is a River: A Black Struggle for Freedom in America* (New York: Harcourt, Brace, Jovanovich, Publishers, 1981), p. 29.
18. Cited in John Winthrop's *Journal*, reprinted in Lorenzo Greene, *The Negro in Colonial New England* (New York: Columbia University Press, 1942), p. 257. See also pp. 265–66.
19. Bennet, *Before the Mayflower*, p. 44.
20. See Helen Tunnicliff Catterall, ed., *Judicial Cases Concerning American Slavery and the Negro*, 4 vols. (Washington, D.C.: The Carnegie Institution, 1926).
21. Quoted in Edgar Pennington, "Thomas Bray's Associates and Their Work Among the Negroes," in *Proceedings of the American Antiquarian Society* new series, 48 (1938): 333.
22. The reference to "saucy" is from Raboteau, who adds that slaves "would begin to think themselves equal to white folks." Albert J. Raboteau, *Slave Religion* (New York: Oxford University Press, 1978), p. 102.
23. This form of architecture with built-in pit was first brought to my attention by an ITC student from Alabama. Examples still exist in a few churches in Alabama.
24. Anthony Browder, *Nile Valley Contributions to Civilization: Exploiting the Myths* (Washington, D.C.: The Institute of Karmic Guidance, 1992), 86.

3. Worship in the Invisible Institution

1. Leonard E. Barret, *Soul Force: African Heritage and Afro-American Religion* (New York: Anchor Press /Doubleday, 1974), p. 96.
2. Robert Anderson, *From Slavery to Affluence: Memories of Robert Anderson, Ex-Slave*, ed. Daisy Anderson Leonard (Steamboat Springs, Colo.: The Steamboat Pilot, 1927), pp. 22–23. See also Frederika Bremer, *The Homes in the New World: Impressions of America*, trans. Mary Howitt (New York: Negro Universities Press, 1968), vol. I, pp. 289–90; Harriet A. Jacobs, *Incidents in the Life of a Slave Girl*, ed. Jean Fagan Yellin (Cambridge, Mass.: Harvard University Press), pp. 63–79.

3. Albert Raboteau, *Slave Religion and the "Invisible Institution" in the Antebellum South* (New York: Oxford University Press, 1980), p. 216. See also George P. Rawick, ed., *The American Slave: A Composite Autobiography,* 31 vols. (Westport, Conn.: Greenwood Press, 1972, 1978), vol. 16, Tennessee, p. 34; vol. 6, Alabama, p. 40; vol. 11, Arkansas, p. 295.

4. Rawick, *The American Slave,* vol. 4, Texas, p. 198.

5. Peter Randolph, *Sketches of Slave Life or Illustrations of the Peculiar Institution,* 2nd ed. (Philadelphia: Rhistoric Publications, 1969), pp. 30–31. Randolph, a slave in Prince George County, Virginia, was freed in 1847.

6. See especially John S. Mbiti, *The Prayers of African Religion* (Maryknoll, N.Y.: Orbis Books, 1975); and Aylward Shorter, *Prayers in the Religious Traditions of Africa* (New York: Oxford University Press, 1975).

7. Melva W. Costen, "The Prayer Tradition of Black Americans," *Reformed Liturgy and Music* XV 2 (Spring 1981): 86.

8. Ibid., p. 89.

9. Harold Carter, *The Prayer Tradition of Black People* (Valley Forge: Judson Press, 1976), p. 55. See also Richard Bowyer, Betty L. Hart, and Charlotte A. Meade, *Prayer in the Black Tradition* (Nashville: The Upper Room, 1986). In addition to a general overview of prayer in the Black tradition, the authors have provided a collection of prayers by contemporary African Americans and prayer in Black literature.

10. Cited in Rawick, *The American Slave,* vol. 4, Texas, pp. 6–7.

11. Among the significant documentations of the song heritage of African Americans are William Francis Allen et al., *Slave Songs of the United States* (New York: A. Simpson & Co., 1897; reprint edition, New York: Books for Libraries Press, 1971); James H. Cone, *The Spirituals and the Blues* (New York: Seabury Press, 1972); Melva Wilson Costen, *In Spirit and in Truth: The Music of African American Worship* (Louisville: Westminster John Knox, 2004); Melva W. Costen, "Singing Praise to God in African American Worship," in Gayraud S. Wilmore, ed., *African American Religious Studies* (Durham, N.C.: Duke University Press, 1989), pp. 392–403; Dena J. Epstein, *Sinful Tunes and Spirituals: Black Folk Music to the Civil War* (Chicago: University of Illinois Press, 1977); Miles Mark Fisher, *Negro Slave Songs in the United States* (New York: Citadel Press, 1969); Irene V. Jackson, ed., *More Than Dancing: Essays on Afro-American Music and Musicians* (Westport, Conn.: Greenwood Press, 1985); James Weldon Johnson and J. Rosamond Johnson, *The Books of Negro Spirituals* (New York: Viking, 1925); John Lovell, *Black Song: The Forge and the Flame* (New York: Macmillan, 1972); J. Wendell Mapson Jr., *The Ministry of Music in the Black Church* (Valley Forge: Judson Press, 1984); Eileen Southern, *The Music of Black Americans: A History,* 2nd ed. (New York: W. W. Norton & Company, 1983); Jon Michael Spencer, *Protest and Praise: Sacred Music of Black Religion* (Minneapolis: Fortress Press, 1990); Wyatt T. Walker, *"Somebody's Calling My Name": Black Sacred Music and Social Change* (Valley Forge: Judson Press, 1979); John Wesley Work, *American Negro Songs and Spirituals* (New York: Bonanza Books, 1940); John Wesley Work, *Folk Songs of the American Negro* (New York: Negro Universities Press, 1969).

12. See W. E. B. DuBois, *The Souls of Black Folk* (Greenwich, Conn.: Fawcett, 1961; originally published in 1898), p. 181. In the closing chapter of this book, DuBois refers to the slave songs as "sorrow songs" because (for him) they represented "the music of an unhappy people, of the children of disappointment," p. 182.

13. Melva W. Costen, "Singing Praise to God in African American Worship Contexts," p. 393.

14. James H. Cone, *Speaking the Truth* (Grand Rapids: William B. Eerdmans, 1986), p. 25.

15. James H. Cone, *The Spirituals and the Blues* (New York: Seabury Press, 1972), p. 57.

16. Ibid., p. 48.

17. According to the Spirituals examined, slaves seldom drew a line of distinction between Jesus and Moses as deliverers.

18. As indicated in chapter 1, *griot* is a West African term for one who is gifted in the art of communicating wisdom, ideas, historical events, morals, and so on.

19. George T'Ofori Atta Thomas, "The African Inheritance in the Black Church Worship," in Melva W. Costen and Darius L. Swann, eds., *The Black Christian Worship Experience*, rev. ed., Black Church Scholar Series, vol. IV (Atlanta: The ITC Press, 1992), pp. 43–74.
20. See John S. Mbiti, *African Religions and Philosophy* (New York: Anchor/Doubleday, 1970), pp. 248–50. Also Michael C. Kirwen, *The Missionary and the Diviner* (Maryknoll, N.Y.: Orbis Books, 1987), passim.
21. T'Ofori Atta Thomas, "The African Inheritance in the Black Church Worship," p. 71.
22. Quoted in Christopher Hill, *The Century of Revolution, 1603–1714* (New York: Norton, 1966), p. 83. It is possible that Colonel Leath, a superintendent in Memphis, Tennessee, was concerned about this in 1870 when he forbade African Americans to read Scriptures and to pray in the public schools. See A. L. Robinson, "In the Aftermath of Slavery" (Yale University, unpublished undergraduate thesis, 1969), p. 227.
23. Eugene D. Genovese, *Roll, Jordan, Roll: The World the Slaves Made* (New York: Vintage Books, 1976), p. 273.
24. Ibid., p. 275.

4. Praise House Worship

1. John F. Watson, *Methodist Error or Friendly Christian Advice to Those Methodists Who Indulge in Extravagant Religious Emotions and Bodily Exercises*. Quoted in Eileen Southern, ed., "John F. Watson," *Readings in Black American Music* (New York: W. W. Norton, 1983), pp. 62–64.
2. William Francis Allen et al., *Slave Songs of the United States* (New York: A. Simpson & Co., 1867), xii–xiv.
3. Reported in Southern, *Readings in Black American Music*, p. 178.
4. Daniel A. Payne, *Recollections of Seventy Years*, reprint ed. (New York: Arno Press, 1969), pp. 253–57.
5. See Samuel Floyd, *The Power of Black Music* (Oxford: Oxford University Press, 1995). A fascinating study based on the thesis that the circular motion of the "Ring Shout" provides the foundation upon which jazz compositions and performances are structured has been proposed by Samuel Floyd. This is also evidenced in Gospel music performances as well.

5. Rituals, Sacraments, and Ordinances

1. Erwin R. Goodenough, *The Psychology of Religious Experiences* (New York: Basic Books, 1965), p. 8. See also Paul W. Pruyser, *A Dynamic Psychology of Religion* (New York: Harper, 1968), pp. 337–39; and Mircea Eliade, *Images and Symbols*, trans. Philip Mauret (New York: Sheed and Ward, 1968).
2. This concept might have been intended by Duke Ellington in his composition "Come Sunday." See this musical setting in *The United Methodist Hymnal* (Nashville: The United Methodist Publishing House, 1989), number 728.
3. See John S. Mbiti, *Concepts of God in Africa* (New York: Praeger, 1970), pp. 137–38.
4. See Melva W. Costen and Darius L. Swann, eds., *The Black Christian Worship Experience*, rev. ed., Black Church Scholar Series, vol. IV (Atlanta: The ITC Press, 1992), pp. 23–42.
5. See Melville J. Herskovitz, *The Myth of th Negro Past* (Boston: Beacon Press, 1958), pp. 232–35.
6. See Carter G. Woodson, *The History of the Negro Church* (Washington, D.C.: The Associated Publishers, 1972), p. 6.
7. Frank J. Klingberg, ed., *The Carolina Chronicale of Dr. Francis Le Jau, 1706–1717* (Los Angeles: University of California Press, 1956), p. 76.
8. See Faith Vibert, "The Society for the Propagation of the Gospel in Foreign Parts: Its Work for the Negroes in North America Before 1783," *Journal of Negro History* 18, 2 (April 1933): 176. For

further information about catechetical efforts, see also Edgard Legare Pennington, *Thomas Bray's Associates and Their Work Among the Negroes* (Worcester, Mass.: The American Antiquarian Society, 1939).

9. The popularity of this Catechism is attested to by the publishing of ten editions by 1852 and translations into Armenian, Armeno Turkish, and Chinese. It was also used by Episcopalians in the United States.

10. Albert L. Raboteau, *Slave Religion* (New York: Oxford University Press, 1978), p. 126.

11. George P. Rawick, ed., *The American Slave: A Composite Autobiography*, vol. 3 (Westport, Conn.: Greenwood Publishing Company, 1972), "South Carolina," part 3, p. 19.

12. Ibid., vol. 13, "Georgia," part 3, pp. 252–53.

13. See Raymond Morris Bost, "The Reverend John Bachman and the Development of Southern Lutheranism" (Ph.D. dissertation, Yale University, 1963; Ann Arbor, Mich.: University Microfilms), pp. 126, 387.

14. See *Records of St. Mary's Roman Catholic Church*, Diocesan Archives, Charleston, S.C.: "The Private Register of the Reverend Paul Trapier," *Publication of the Dalcho Historical Society of the Diocese of South Carolina*, February 11, 1848. Quoted in Erskine Clarke, *Wrestlin' Jacob* (Atlanta: John Knox Press, 1979), p. 132.

15. Clarke, *Wrestlin' Jacob*, p. 131.

16. See Charles C. Jones, *A Catechism of Scripture, Doctrine, and Practice: For Families and Sabbath Schools, Designed Also for the Oral Instruction of Colored Persons*, 3rd ed. (Savannah: T. Purse and Company, 1845).

17. Sessional Minutes of the Session, Second Presbyterian Church, 1814.

18. The piety exhibited might have been more related to African world views than to that of Christianity.

19. Quoted in Clarke, *Wrestlin' Jacob*, p. 134, from Edward G. Lilly, *Beyond the Burning Bush: First (Scots) Presbyterian Church* (Charleston, S.C.: Garnier & Company, 1971), pp. 14–15.

20. See J. Lansing Burrows, ed., *American Baptist Register for 1852* (Philadelphia: American Baptist Publication Society, 1853), pp. 70–74; James M. Simms, *The First Colored Baptist Church in North America* (Philadelphia: Lippincott, 1888), pp. 63–64. While First African Baptist Church was struggling to be free of the control of the Euro-American Baptist Sunbury Association, they were advised by the Association not to allow the pastor, Andrew Marshall, to preach or administer the ordinances of baptism and the Lord's Supper. With perseverance, the church not only survived, but became a tourist attraction for visitors to the city of Savannah.

21. An attempt of churches to develop guidelines for the marriage of slaves can be found in *Records of Marriages Performed by Reverend Edward Philips, Employed as the Missionary to the Protestant Episcopal Domestic Missionary Society and Subsequently the Minister of St. Steven's Chapel, 1822–1860*, ms. (South Carolina Historical Society); also *Minutes of the Session, Zion Presbyterian Church* (October 25, 1859), pp. 156–58.

22. Pricilla "Mittle" Munnikhuysen Bond, MS Diary, 1858–1865 (Louisiana State University, Saturday, January 4, 1862).

23. Hallowe'en, or Halloween, is a contraction for All Hallows E'en.

24. See Eugene D. Genovese, *Roll, Jordan, Roll: The World the Slaves Made* (New York: Vintage Books, 1974), p. 194.

25. The Spiritual "My Lord, What a Morning" (or Mourning) is associated with this belief.

26. See Elliot P. Skinner, *People and Cultures of Africa* (Garden City, N.Y.: The Doubleday/Natural History Press, 1973), pp. 374–90.

27. William E. Hatcher, *John Jasper: The Unmatched Negro Philosopher and Preacher* (New York: Fleming H. Revell Co., 1908), p. 38.

28. See Melville J. Herskovits and Frances S. Herskovits, *Rebel Destiny Among the Bush Negroes of Dutch Guiana* (New York: McGraw-Hill, 1934), p. 99.

29. See Melville J. Herskovits, *Dahomey: An Ancient West African Kingdom*, vol. 1 (Evanston, Ill.: Northwestern University Press, 1967; reprint of the 1938 edition), p. 374.

30. See *Rules and Regulations of the Brown Fellowship Society Established at Charleston, South Carolina*, 1st November, 1790 (Charleston, S.C.: J. B. Nixon, 1844).

31. These figures were quoted in Clarke, *Wrestlin' Jacob*, p. 137, from Richard C. Wade, *Slavery in the Cities: The South 1820–1860* (New York: Oxford University Press, 1967), pp. 169–70.

32. See Luther P. Jackson, "The Early Strivings of the Negro in Virginia," *Journal of Negro History* 24 (1940): 33.

6. Origins and Practices of African American Denominations and Congregations

1. See references to Black churches in C. Eric Lincoln and Lawrence H. Mamiya, *The Black Church in the African American Experience* (Durham, N.C.: Duke University Press, 1990); Wyatt Tee Walker, *"Somebody's Calling My Name": Black Sacred Music and Social Change* (Valley Forge: Judson Press, 1979); and James H. Cone, *Speaking the Truth* (Grand Rapids: William B. Eerdmans, 1986).

2. Richard Wright, *12 Million Voices: A Folk History of the Negro in the United States* (New York: Viking Press, 1941), p. 131.

3. Victor W. Turner, *The Ritual Process: Structures and Anti-Structures* (Ithaca, N.Y.: Cornell University Press, 1969), p. 129.

4. See Mechal Sobel, *Trabelin' On* (Princeton, N.J.: Princeton University Press, 1979), p. 159.

5. Bert J. Loewenberg and Ruth Bogin, eds., *Black Women in Nineteenth Century America* (University Park, Pa.: Pennsylvania State University, 1976), p. 127.

6. Ibid., pp. 135–41.

7. Jean McMahon Humez, *Gifts of Power: The Writings of Rebecca Jackson, Black Visionary, Shaker Eldress* (Amherst: University of Massachusetts Press, 1981).

8. Loewenberg et al., eds., *Black Women in Nineteenth Century America*, pp. 142–73.

9. Austa Malinda French, *Slavery in South Carolina and the Ex-Slaves; or the Port Royal Mission* (New York: Negro Universities Press, 1969), p. 100.

10. For a chronological index of founding dates and locations of Black Baptist churches, see Mechal Sobel, *Trabelin' On*, pp. 250–356.

11. Carter G. Woodson, *The History of the Negro Church*, 3rd ed. (Washington, D.C.: The Associated Publishers, 1972), p. 35.

12. See Lincoln and Mamiya, *The Black Church in the African American Experience*, p. 416.

13. For a brief composite of historical data concerning some of these churches, see ibid., pp. 20–91.

14. See especially St. Clair Drake and Horace Cayton, *Black Metropolis: A Study of Negro Life in the North*, vol. 2, rev. ed. (New York: Harper & Row,1962), p. 424; E. Franklin Frazier and C. Eric Lincoln, *The Negro Church in America: The Black Church Since Frazier* (New York: Schocken Books, 1975), pp. 78-81, 85-86; Gunnar Myrdal, *An American Dilemma: The Negro Problem and Modern Democracy* (New York: Harper & Row, 1962), p. 928; Hart M. Nelsen and Anne Kusener Nelsen, *Black Churches in the Sixties* (Lexington: University of Kentucky Press, 1975), pp. 8–13; Lincoln and Mamiya, *The Black Church in the African American Experience*, pp. 10–16; Anthony Odum, "A Reappraisal of the Social and Political Participation of Negroes," *American Journal of Sociology* 72 (July 1966): 33; and Charles Silberman, *Crisis in Black and White* (New York: Random House, 1964), p. 144.

15. Nelsen and Nelsen, *Black Churches in the Sixties*, pp. 8–13.

16. Lincoln and Mamiya, *The Black Church in the African American Experience*, pp. 11–16.

17. Melva Wilson Costen, "Black Worship in a Small Town," *Liturgy* 6,1 (Summer 1986): 15–23.

18. Information shared from the oral history of Mound Bayou, Mississippi, by Ms. Addie Peterson.

7. How Music, Preaching, and Prayer Shape Contemporary African American Worship

1. See Riggins R. Earl, "Under Their Own Vine and Fig Tree: The Ethics of Social and Spiritual Hospitality in Black Church Worship," in Melva W. Costen and Darius L. Swann, eds., *The Black Christian Worship Experience*, rev. ed., Black Church Scholar Series, vol. IV (Atlanta: The ITC Press, 1992), pp. 181–93.

2. Consultations on African American Worship Traditions Research Project, Interdenominational Theological Center, Atlanta, Georgia, Melva W. Costen and Darius Swann, Co-chairpersons. The book *The Black Christian Worship Experience*, previously cited, resulted from the first consultation.

3. Two editions were printed in 1801, the first by John Ormond, the second by T. L. Plowman.

4. See the table of contents reprinted in Eileen Southern, *Readings in Black American Music* (New York: W. W. Norton, 1983), pp. 53–54.

5. Ibid., p. 52.

6. Quoted in John Lovell Jr., *Black Song: The Forge and the Flame* (New York: Macmillan, 1972), p. 106.

7. Radical Spirituals include "Joshua Fit the Battle of Jericho," "Singin' with a Sword in My Hand," and "I'm on the Battlefield for My Lord."

8. Lovell, *Black Song*, p. 193.

9. The first rule of governance for the Organization of the Society of Negroes states that "between two Prayers, a Psalm shall be sung."

10. Wyatt Tee Walker, *"Somebody's Calling My Name": Black Sacred Music and Social Change* (Valley Forge: Judson Press, 1979), p. 98.

11. There is great similarity in the hymnody of the Black Baptist denominations. Initial hymnals were closely modeled after those published by their Euro-American counterparts. It is also of interest that *The New National Baptist Hymnal*, published in 1977, is widely used across denominational lines. The Christian Methodist Episcopal Church (CME) adopted it as the official denominational hymnal in 1987 by merely changing the cover and title page, adding one song composed by a CME bishop, interchanging the two opening hymns, and adding the rituals of the CME Church.

12. Michael W, Harris, *The Rise of the Gospel Blues: The Music of Thomas Andrew Dorsey in the Urban Church* (New York: Oxford University Press, 1992), p. 209.

13. Tony Heilbut, *The Gospel Sound* (New York: Simon and Schuster, 1971), p. 11.

14. See especially Henry Mitchell, *Celebration and Experience in Preaching* (Nashville: Abingdon Press, 1990).

15. See J. Alfred Smith, *Preach On!* (Nashville: Broadman Press, 1984). This volume deals with preaching as a poetic art form.

16. These are the opening words often heard in traditional Black prayers.

17. *Lex credendi (est) lex* orandi—"doctrine determines worship"—is the theological adage applicable to this process. In African American worship there is more of an interplay of reciprocal influence, with prayer or what one prays (*orandi*) being the basic determining factor for elements of worship.

18. This matter and the use of keyboard instruments for accompaniment resulted in the withdrawal of some of the dissident members from the Church.

19. *The Book of Worship of the African Methodist Episcopal Church* (Nashville: The A.M.E. Sunday School Union, 1984); *The AMEC Bicentennial Hymnal* (Nashville: The African Methodist Episcopal Church, 1884), pp. 785–804.

20. The rituals of the Church are included in the back of the *A.M.E. Zion Hymnal* (Charlotte, N.C.: A.M.E. Zion Publishing House, 1957).

21. *Church of God in Christ Official Manual* (Memphis: Church of God in Christ Publishing House, 1973).

22. Quoted in Southern, *Readings in Black American Music*, pp. 62–63; from John F. Watson, *Methodist Error or Friendly Christian Advice to Those Methodists Who Indulge in Extravagant Religious Emotions and Bodily Exercises* (Trenton, N.J.: D. and E. Fenton, 1819), pp. 28–31.

23. Donald G. Mathews, *Religion in the Old South* (Chicago: The University of Chicago Press, 1977), p. 185.
24. Ibid., p. 186.

8. Worship as Empowerment

1. Gayraud S. Wilmore, *Black Religion and Black Radicalism,* 2nd ed. (Maryknoll, N.Y.: Orbis Books, 1983), p. 220.
2. Ivan Illich, *The Church, Change and Development* (New York: Herder and Herder, 1970), p. 19.
3. See James H. Cone, *Speaking the Truth* (Grand Rapids: Eerdmans, 1986), pp. 18–19.
4. See Edward P. Wimberly, *African American Pastoral Care* (Nashville: Abingdon Press, 1991), p. 15. In this valuable resource, Wimberly, an African American professor of psychology and pastoral care, demonstrates a narrative approach to pastoral care in the Black church, which links persons in need to God's ongoing, unfolding story.
5. Ibid., p. 26.
6. Ibid., p. 25.
7. Howard Thurman, *The Creative Encounter: An Interpretation of Religion and Social Witness,* reprint ed. (Richmond, Ind.: Friends United Press, 1972), pp. 22–27.
8. See William H. Willimon, *Worship as Pastoral Care* (Nashville: Abingdon Press, 1979), p. 57.
9. Three of the most familiar insurrections were those of Gabriel Prosser (1800), Denmark Vessey (1822), and Nat Turner (1831). The account of more than two hundred slave revolts, some of which were related to religious gatherings, has been recorded in Herbert Aptheker, *American Negro Slave Revolts* (New York: International Publishers, 1943).
10. Notable examples are the *Psalter Hymnal* (Christian Reformed Church, 1987); the *Baptist Hymnal* (Southern Baptist, 1991); *The Presbyterian Hymnal* (1990); and *The United Methodist Hymnal* (1989). Separate hymnals containing racial ethnic songs have also been published by The United Methodist Church. African American hymnals have been published by The Episcopal Church (*Lift Every Voice,* 1981) and the Roman Catholic Church (*Lead Me, Guide Me,* 1987). Nondenominational hymnals that have included a significant number of African American songs are *The Hymnal for Worship and Celebration* (Waco, Tex.: Word Music, 1986) and *The Worshiping Church* (Carol Stream, Ill.: Hope Publishing Company, 1990).
11. Incorporating African American songs in the main body of hymnals according to theological and seasonal headings rather than by racial-ethnic categories reflects a rather recent trend in hymnal publications.
12. A few resources include the outstanding works by Henry H. Mitchell, *Black Preaching* (Philadelphia: Lippincott, 1970); *The Recovery of Preaching* (San Francisco: Harper, 1975); *Celebration and Experience in Preaching* (Nashville: Abingdon Press, 1990); and numerous articles, including "Narrative in the Black Tradition," in Richard L. Eslinger, ed., *A New Hearing* (Nashville: Abingdon Press, 1987), pp. 39–63; James E. Massey, *Designing the Sermon* (Nashville: Abingdon Press, 1980); Warren H. Stewart, *Interpreting God's Word in Black Preaching* (Valley Forge: Judson Press, 1984); and Samuel Proctor and William D. Watley, *Sermons from the Black Pulpit* (Valley Forge: Judson Press, 1984).
13. Notable among published sermons by Black women are Ella Mitchell, ed., *Those Preachin' Women* (Valley Forge: Judson Press, 1985); *Those Preaching Women* (Valley Forge: Judson Press, 1988); and *Women: To Preach or Not to Preach* (Valley Forge: Judson Press, 1991).
14. Mitchell, *The Recovery of Preaching,* p. 33.
15. Mitchell, *Celebration and Experience in Preaching,* p. 61.
16. See especially Charles Rice, "Preaching as Story," in Eslinger, *A New Hearing,* pp. 17–37; Eugene Lowry, "Narrative and the Sermonic Plot," ibid., pp. 64–94; Eugene Lowry, *The Homiletical Plot: The Sermon as Narrative Art Form* (Atlanta: John Knox Press, 1980); Eugene Lowry, *How to*

Preach a Parable (Nashville: Abingdon Press, 1989); John Dominic Crossan, *The Dark Interval: Toward a Theology of Story* (Allen, Tex.: Argus Communications, 1975); Richard A. Jensen, *Telling the Story* (Minneapolis: Augsburg, 1980).

17. Denise Lardner Carmody and John Tully Carmody, *Prayer in World Religions* (Maryknoll, N.Y.: Orbis Books, 1990), pp. 143–44.

INDEX

Carter, Harold, 31
catechesis, baptism and, 20, 22, 46, 48–50
catechism, learning, 18, 49
Catechism . . . for the Oral Instruction of Colored Persons, 50, 133n9
Catholic Church, 12, 15, 46, 50, 52, 137n10
cemeteries, colored, 62
"Certainly Lord," 52
chants, 83, 86, 88, 97
children, 7, 19, 60–61
choirs, 77, 85, 91, 123
Christian Methodist Episcopal Church (CME), 73, 88, 97–98, 136n11
Christian Methodist Episcopal Church Book of Rituals and Aids to Worship, 98
Christianity, 10, 15, 16, 130n3. *See also* Judeo-Christian traditions
church(es), 19, 22, 35, 77, 103, 131n23. *See also specific churches/denominations*
Church of England, 49
Church of God in Christ, 100
Church of God in Christ Official Manual, 100
civil rights movement, 75, 90
Clarke, Erskine, 52–53
Clement, 2
CME. *See* Christian Methodist Episcopal Church
code words, 12, 29
coffins, 59–61
COGIC. *See* Church of God in Christ
Collection of Hymns and Spiritual Songs from Various Authors, A (Allen), 81–82
colonial America, 14, 16–22
"Come Sunday," 133n2
commitment, 125
communication
    forms of, 13–14
    with God, 32–33, 42, 68–69
    through symbols, 6
communion, 52–54, 98
community, 2–3, 43, 118–19
    burials and, 59
    core beliefs and, 5–8
    as extended family, 1, 5, 9
    identity and, 7, 75, 76, 130n12
    Invisible Institution and, 26, 29–30
    kinship and, 5, 8–12, 51, 78, 79
    wholeness and, 7, 66–68, 94
Cone, James, 33–34
confession
    prayer of, 122
    of sins, 51, 80, 98, 113

congregations, 3, 11–12, 65–78. *See also* African American congregations
conversion, 2, 15, 21. *See also* baptism
Cooper, Thomas, 82–83
Cooper-Lewter, Nicholas C., 7
cosmic rhythm, 6, 22
cosmology, African, 5–6, 23
creeds, 2, 7–8, 97, 98
Cyprian, 2
Cyril, 2

dancing, 19, 36, 41–43, 59
death, 51. *See also* burials; funerals
Decalogue, 97
denominational polity, 2, 77, 121
denominations
    African American vs. Euro-American, 76–77, 80, 85–86, 97, 98, 101–2, 136n11
    differences in/between, 3–4, 11–12, 66
    diversity among congregations and, 11–12, 75
    Euro-American, African American congregations in, 66, 68–69, 70, 103
    origin of separate, 70–75
    origins and practices of, 65–78
diakonia, 107, 113
Dialectical Model, 75–77
Didymus, 2
Dionysius, 2
dirt, sprinkling of, 60
discipleship, invitation to, 95, 99, 124–25
Dorsey, Thomas A., 89–90
"double" or "dual" expressions, 12
doxologies, 88, 97
"Dr. Watts," 40, 87
drums, 19
DuBois, W. E. B., 32, 132n12
durante vita (perpetual bondage), 20

economics, 15, 19–20, 22, 46, 76
ecumenicism, 77, 115
education, 76, 77. *See also* schools
Edwards, Anderson, 31–32
Elizabeth (preacher), 69
Ellington, Duke, 133n2
empowerment, 1, 7, 10
    historical foundations of, 106–8
    psychological, 108–11
    worship as, 105–26
Episcopal Church, 11, 52, 71–73, 133n9, 137n10